ORIENTAL
RUGS
IN
NEEDLEPOINT

ORIENTAL RUGS IN NEEDLEPOINT

10 CHARTED DESIGNS

SUSAN
SCHOENFELD
KALISH

 VAN NOSTRAND REINHOLD COMPANY

New York   Cincinnati   Toronto   London   Melbourne

Also by Susan Schoenfeld Kalish
Pattern Design for Needlepoint and Patchwork

Copyright © 1982 by Susan Schoenfeld Kalish
Library of Congress Catalog Card Number 81–11704
ISBN 0–442–27420–3

Published by Van Nostrand Reinhold Company
135 West 50th Street, New York, NY 10020, U.S.A.

Van Nostrand Reinhold Limited
1410 Birchmount Road
Scarborough, Ontario M1P 2E7, Canada

Van Nostrand Reinhold Australia Pty. Ltd.
17 Queen Street
Mitcham, Victoria 3132, Australia

Van Nostrand Reinhold Company Limited
Molly Millars Lane
Wokingham, Berkshire, England

16 15 14 13 12 11 10 9 8 7 6 5 4 3 2 1

Library of Congress Cataloging in Publication Data

Kalish, Susan Schoenfeld.
    Oriental rugs in needlepoint.

    Bibliography: p.
    Includes index.
    1. Canvas embroidery.   2. Rugs, Oriental.   I. Title.
TT778.C3K354   746.7′4   81–11704
ISBN 0–442–27420–3   AACR2

CONTENTS

PREFACE

When I began needlepointing my first Oriental rug, I thought I had a time limit. I was pregnant and looked forward to completing both of these first major "projects" in the same nine-month term. How little I knew then that far from completing something, I was just beginning two very deep involvements!

Previously, I had researched geometric motifs, including those from Oriental rugs. But I knew the motifs individually, rather than in their role within the large designs that were their source. I think that the new approach has helped me to appreciate all the more the wonderful resolution with which a few motifs are incorporated into an Oriental rug design to achieve a feeling of complexity by a true economy of means.

Shortly after I decided to start a large needlepoint rug (maybe the result of an unconscious association between babies and carpets, as in the classic baby picture), I happened to go to a preview exhibition at the soon-to-be-opened Islamic galleries of The Metropolitan Museum of Art in New York. There, among other masterworks, I saw a Bergama rug (my adaptation is shown on the back of the jacket) that impressed me deeply. As a painter as well as a needleworker, I had seen many solutions to the basic problems of organizing shapes and colors on a flat surface, but few so satisfying. Here was evident the simplicity that comes only from intelligence, the kind that includes and resolves opposites. The design was bold but subtle. There was no "empty" space—the area was filled with motifs, yet it was not a confusing design. Emotional and visual associations came to mind as I looked at it: the night sky, animals, power, rhythm, vitality—associations that seemed to me to connect with the life forming within me. The greatest pleasure I could think of at that moment would have been to roll that rug up and take it home with me. Since that was out of the question, I decided upon the next best thing: to stitch it in needlepoint.

To do so I needed to make a graph of the rug. Accordingly, I bought a large roll of graph paper. The first thing I discovered was the obvious: admiring it was a lot easier than charting it. I found that I had to learn its visual language, which was unfamiliar to my Western eyes. It was like entering a new world of forms and colors. I was not yet used to looking at the ends of the knots that form the pile—akin to the dots in some impressionist paintings—and perceiving how they made up the construction of the rug.

From the rug and a color reproduction I did drawings, took notes, and made color notations. I worked from observation, memory, feeling, and intuition. And I began to make my interpretations. The work that followed provided many hours of relaxation during the first year after my child was born, when much of my time was spent at home.

The making of that rug blossomed into an interest in all Oriental rugs, especially in how the rugs were designed and made. I searched books for insights into the design of Oriental rugs, but they were vague and literary. My most reliable sources of information were the rugs themselves. I attended exhibitions at auction galleries and found them invaluable. In a museum, the rule "look, but don't touch" is strictly enforced. But before an auction of rugs, even rugs of museum quality, the prospective buyer is expected to examine them as closely as he or she wishes. Knowing the feel of a rug is important. And if you wish to coax it to reveal its secrets, it is essential that you have an opportunity to look at its back. There the knots are visible, and you can count them to see how they make up the design. Sometimes it is also possible to see the knots on the front of an old rug in which the pile has worn away—such rugs actually bear a resemblance to a needlepoint and helped me to visualize my adaptations. If you have ever attended a rug auction in New York and seen a woman with a pad of graph paper in one hand obsessively counting the knots on the back of rugs, that was probably me.

In adapting that first rug to a needlepoint design, I became aware of the importance of the almost-always-present outline: it separates the colors, often appears to soften the edges of the shapes, and is a means of delineating those shapes. To find the dimensions of a motif, I simply had to count the knots of the outline. But first I had to find a clear example of the motif, since there were always variations of the knot count. Sometimes it was necessary to compare more than one motif within a rug to arrive at the most generically representative one. I found that the longer I looked, the clearer the design became—all the information I needed was there to be seen, and what at first seemed so complex, progressively revealed its stunning simplicity. With only a very few motifs and colors, imaginative combinations and variations were achieved.

In stitching my rug and studying the original I also discovered that the colors of an Oriental rug come made from natural vegetable dyes that produce deep, rich (sometimes irregular) colors; the colors are not really equivalent to those of chemically dyed yarns available today. Therefore, I had to tread very carefully when choosing colors. The white of the rugs, I found, was not the light, ultrabright white of today, but a grayish color. A color that appeared to be brown turned out to be a violet on closer examination. Sometimes a color could not be matched at all but had to be achieved by blending two or more yarn colors. When seen separately, most rug colors would appear rather subdued to modern, Western eyes, but together in a rug they are vibrant and beautiful. Also, because of the pile, the direction and quality of the light and the tactile quality of the wool greatly influence the appearance of the colors.

When I eventually gave my adaptations to friends to stitch, I was elated to find that, although they were of necessity more regular than the originals, the interpretations were close to them in character; the spirit and feeling were retained. This is due in part, I think, to the fact that I have seen each carpet (or one very closely related) for which I have made a chart and color equivalents.

Many of my actions in re-creating these rugs have echoed those of the original weaver, with whom, in my imagination, I have come to form what I think of as a sympathetic relationship. I have tried to put myself in her place before the design existed and to retrace her steps in creating it. In so doing, I feel that I have developed a liking for the person herself, or at least for that quality which she poured so freely and energetically into her work, and which took up by far the greatest part of her waking life.

I have, therefore, become rather skeptical of the value of pattern books that attempt to water down the designs, "color coordinate" them to fit into decorator color schemes, or chart them with every last detail precisely graphed and color coded. Despite their seeming complexity, Oriental rug patterns are simple enough so that the outlines may be learned from the charts and then worked in color with one's own variations. This is, in fact, the way the original weavers passed the patterns on, teaching the knot count to their children (often they had no chart at all, or only a very fragmentary one). I think of the designs as songs, originally learned at a mother's knee, which are made one's own in the singing; it is not necessary or desirable to change them consciously to make them personal. So, too, with these rugs. They exist in themselves as autonomous worlds of color and shape. Any good Oriental rug will look well in any setting.

In creating each original rug, the weaver used her knowledge of craft, her judgment, intuition, and heritage. I have tried to bring what I could of these qualities to interpreting the originals. I hope that you will stitch one of these rugs in this spirit and experience the pleasure that working and having it can bring.

ACKNOWLEDGMENTS

I would like to thank my husband, Howard Kalish, and my good friend Mila Ahern for their patient help and useful suggestions in writing the manuscript and my father, Phil Schoenfeld, for all the work he put into the drawings in this book.

To all those who speedily and cheerfully stitched the sample rugs go my gratitude and appreciation: Norma Braverman, Selwyn Cooper, Mae Eisenberg, Jane Goldstein, Jerry Levine, Marie Love, Elinor Migdal, Nancy Migdal, Lillian Schoenfeld, and Shirley Wiesen.

I would also like to thank the Islamic Department of The Metropolitan Museum of Art for allowing me to see rugs that were not on public display.

INTRODUCTION

This book explores the world of the Oriental rug through the medium of needlepoint. The true Oriental rug is, of course, worked on a loom; the ten rug patterns provided have been adapted for needlepoint—an easy, enjoyable stitchery technique that produces exquisite and durable results. Though the technique is the same as for any ordinary needlepoint, the result is far from ordinary. The designs in this book are those of classic Oriental rugs, and together they form an elegant collection of Turkish and Caucasian designs that reveal to the modern viewer the creativity of yesterday's rug weavers. Because they are particularly well suited to needlepoint, two Shirvan and two Kazak rugs from the Caucasus and three classic and three country Turkish rugs have been included. Each rug design was chosen for its own special appeal and because it was the best available example of its type. The selection chosen also reflects a shift in taste from the ornate designs of Persian carpets toward the bold geometry and rough drawn charm of Russian folk and Turkish country rugs. To convey the proper spirit, great care has been taken to make these needlepoint adaptations as faithful as possible to the originals, with the same subdued color and authentic detail.

This book is intended for both beginning and more experienced needleworkers. It is especially well suited to the experienced person in search of sophisticated, challenging design. The Transylvanian Rug (color plate C-4), for example, will give ambitious needleworkers an opportunity to demonstrate needlepoint artistry and rugmaking skills. A pair of flowering vases graces the center of the field; elaborate Arabesques decorate each corner. An outer border accented with Arabesques and stars completes the design for a rug that measures 48 inches by 66 inches (121.9 cm by 167.7 cm). Beyond the ten complete rug designs included, more than fifty individual design elements, such as border and field motifs that can be used alone or in combination, offer the skilled needleworker a variety of new project ideas.

These same fifty individual design elements can be used by anyone who does not wish to commit him/herself to making a complete rug, either because of a reluctance to spend the amount of time or money required or because, as a beginner, he/she feels a need to acquire a certain degree of skill, experience, and self-confidence before approaching a larger undertaking. If you fall into the latter category, starting small—using one or some of the design elements in a seven-inch square from which you fashion a pincushion, needlecase, or belt—may be the right approach for you. On the other hand, if you are a bit more adventurous, you can complete a rug from the start, since the fundamental basket-weave stitch is explained and illustrated in a manner that will enable any beginner to master it. The Shirvan Rug design is ideal for a first rug project. It's a stunning folk rug with floral motifs set in diagonal rows between small white squares on a blue background. All the information necessary to stitch this (or any of the other extraordinary rugs in the book) can be found in the following pages; all needed materials are described and tips for purchasing them economically are provided. Technical instructions for stitching, blocking, and finishing are given in detail. Graphs show the designs clearly, and the accompanying instructions indicate how you can most easily stitch them on your canvas. Color keys and color suggestions are also given. You are told how to display and care for your rug to preserve its original beauty.

The person who is reluctant to commit time to making a complete rug may be surprised to learn that the carpets from which the designs in this book were adapted were made entirely by hand, for the most part by women and children. A good weaver would have tied from nine hundred to one thousand knots per hour; a fast needlepointer can do a like number of stitches—enough to fill a three-by-three inch square of #10 canvas. Using this as a basis for computation, the smallest rug in this book, less than nine square feet (25 inches by $38\frac{1}{2}$ inches on #8 mesh), could have been stitched in approximately 70 hours. The largest, more than twenty-six square feet (49 inches by 78 inches), could have been done in about 350 hours. Working at their own convenience and for relaxation, the people who stitched the rugs in this book did so in approximately one to one-and-a-half years (of course, there were variations in rug size). Included in this group of very busy people were two male executives who run their own businesses and the chief surgical nurse in a large urban hospital. One talented needlepointer among them, who had more time than the others, finished her large and complicated rug in nine months.

These people found, as I believe others will, that the process itself is part of the reward. We often look for an excuse to needlepoint, just because we find it relaxing to let the cares of the day dissolve in the rhythm of the stitching. Just as we do not wish an entertaining book or movie to be over too quickly, so a project such as a rug can sustain our interest and enhance our enjoyment of the stitching process just because it *is* long-lasting. Once we establish our rhythm of working, we soon find that it proceeds at a pleasant pace. The design is never really complete until the last stitch of the border is done. During the process we can watch it grow and unfold like a story that is difficult to put down. We begin to look forward to the time of day when we can take it up once more.

Though true Orientals (hand-knotted, pile rugs) bring enormous prices, sometimes in excess of fifty thousand dollars, a needlepoint rug of good design is a thing of value in itself. There is a long tradition of needlemade rugs; they appear in galleries and at auctions and are collected by individuals and museums. In the Victoria and Albert Museum in London, for example, there is a seventeenth-century needlepoint interpretation of an Oriental rug. A needlepoint rug is a piece of fine craftsmanship that will last at least a lifetime. Seen in this light, the cost of materials needed to make one of the rugs in this book—while high in its own right—will seem small. It is difficult to give precise figures because of fluctuations in the cost of materials and variations in prices depending upon where and in what quantities materials are bought. Costs can be kept to a minimum by buying yarn by the pound. In 1981 prices, the smallest rug in this book could have been made for under sixty dollars; the largest could have cost approximately two hundred dollars.

Most of the originals of these needlepoint adaptations are in museums; the rest are in important private collections. They have been cataloged, studied, carefully preserved, and restored. When, at infrequent intervals, rugs of this quality are sold, they bring staggering prices. The basic reason for this goes beyond their rarity or their history: it is simply that they are breathtakingly beautiful. For most people the only way to own such an artifact—which is so far from the commonplace and which effortlessly and elegantly becomes the focal point of a room, lifting it to a higher level—is to make it for themselves. If you choose to be one of these owners, I believe you will find that through the time-honored activity of making something fine and lasting with your own hands your time will have been well spent. Good stitching!

1. MATERIALS AND TECHNIQUES

A Place to Work

The first needlepoint I ever did was a tiny sampler of small geometric pattern. I remember being able to take it anywhere—once I even stitched it in a subway car when the lights were out. This portability is certainly a positive quality.

But I would not give up making a rug for lack of convenience. A rug is cumbersome but manageable. The key is to have a comfortable place to work that is, if possible, constant from one session to the next. You can use a frame to hold the rug or a table to support the bulk of its weight. It can be rolled up, or simply draped over your lap (particularly on a cold night). One needlepointer stitched while lying in bed watching television, the rug covering her legs. Another invented and built his own frame for holding the rug while it was being stitched. The rug will not be harmed by folding, and it can be stored this way, or even worked with only the small area you need unfolded. You should have a good light when working, with its source coming over the shoulder opposite the hand that is stitching.

The rug, even when incomplete, makes a nice display; you can leave it on a frame or table where it can be seen. In fact, Oriental rugs were commonly used as table covers in Europe and early America and are depicted thus in many paintings.

An accessible and comfortable work place is important in a psychological as well as physical sense. You should look forward to the time when you are stitching as relaxation, a time for settling into your own snug little nest. Awaiting you there will be the basket containing your yarn and a comfortable chair that supports yet gives free play to your stitching arm. There you can fall easily into the unhurried rhythm of the work and enjoy its steady progress.

The Yarn and Its Colors

No one who loves color can fail to respond to the splashy profusion of most yarn shops—the bright sky blues, the yellows, reds, and oranges all competing for attention. Amid this splendor, if one were to ask for the yarn for a typical Oriental rug, the clerk would not reach for those colors that immediately catch the eye. The palette of Oriental rugs and their adaptations in this book are based on subtle colors traditionally obtained from natural sources; they are earthier and more subdued than colors from chemical dyes. Almost hidden by the fire-engine reds, lemon yellows, brilliant

greens, our color range waits. The dyers who created these colors were masters of their art. Their formulas were carefully guarded secrets that were passed from generation to generation. The dyes were made of herbs, roots, insects, and other natural sources.

Here are descriptions of the colors of the basic Oriental rug palette and their original raw materials.

Red is a warm, earthy, bricklike color. Its shades range from somewhat pink to rust. It is the color most often used for the background in the field (the rectangle inside the border framework). Though most Westerners would probably not consider red a background hue, the mellow tones used in Oriental rugs show the motifs and patterns very well and complement the other colors. Red was most often made from the root of the madder plant. An insect called cochineal produced a red, also called cochineal, of a more purple hue.

Blue is made from indigo plants. It is not a bright blue, but a deep, rich, nocturnal shade. The color ranges from dark blue to a lighter grayed blue.

Yellow can be any tone from rather dark ocher to gold to a light yellow-tan. It is never a sunny or lemon yellow. There are many different yellows because they come from many sources: various flower petals, the stalks and leaves of flowers, sumac, saffron, and others.

Violet, green, and orange are usually mixtures of the primary hues mentioned above. Violet is a brown-gray purple, which you might actually think of as a brown or gray when seen by itself. Green is never acidic, or yellow-green, but a deep verdant color such as one might discover in a dark, shady grove. It represents the color of the Prophet for some Islamic sects and is rarely used in large areas in Turkish rugs. When not created by a mixture of blue and yellow, green can be obtained from ripe turmeric berries or buckthorn. Orange is a salmonlike tone, not at all like the color of the fruit.

Ivory, brown, and brown-black were usually the natural, undyed wool of the sheep. Since the dark tones tend to fade, however, they were often dyed as well, the brown with a dye derived from walnut shells or oak bark. The darker brown-black comes from iron oxide, which is corrosive; areas knotted with that color are often more worn than other areas in old rugs. Ivory, the lightest tone, is the undyed wool of the sheep. It is darker, grayer, more organic in tone than pure white, which can only be obtained by bleaching the wool and never appears in Oriental rugs.

I never cease to be amazed at how these colors, which might seem dull separately, can suddenly appear to be the most luminous primary hues when combined in a rug. One of the best ways to learn about color harmony is to juxtapose various skeins of yarn. Matching colors for an Oriental rug is an object lesson in how the masters did it. On this point I can cite no less authority than the great painter Eugene Delacroix, who was known especially as a colorist. One day he was seen playing with some skeins of wool, putting them together, separating and intertwining them, and achieving some striking color combinations. As he did so, he commented that some of the most beautiful pictures he had seen were certain Oriental rugs.

In an Oriental rug the colors rarely appear consistent. One batch of dyed wool was not the same as the next. Natural sources and processes for making the dyes and the yarn were subject to many variables. Their effects appear in the rug as subtle variations in color along horizontal rows, following the weave. Called *abrash*, this type of variation occurs because of the way Oriental rugs were made, and it enhances their visual interest. Also, the wool has often faded and worn over the years, sometimes differently in different parts of a single rug. To my eye, these variations only add to the richness of the color. Rather than being flat as a freshly painted wall, each color resonates with a jewellike quality, with deeps and lights that seem to impart an inner glow.

Blending Colors

The subtle, natural colors that were used originally do not necessarily find their equivalents in the chemically dyed yarn we use today. A good way to match the original colors and to re-create the effect of color variation is to mix single strands of Persian yarn; this is how rug restorers match colors for the old pieces they repair. Mixing is done by removing one of the three strands and replacing it with a slightly different shade of the same hue.

The rugs in this book were all made with Paternayan Persian yarn, and the color numbers given are for that brand. Where colors were mixed in the sample rugs, a *principal* and one or more *auxiliary* colors are given. In the color charts the number of the principal color is printed in boldface type, the auxiliaries in lighter type. The principal color is the basic color of the area and should predominate. The auxiliaries are used for variation. If you do not wish to go to the extra trouble that mixing entails, it is not absolutely necessary. Simply use the principal color only, without the auxiliaries. The design will be the same, but the color effect will be uniform rather than varied.

If you do choose to mix colors, think of each color as a mixture of the principal and its auxiliary, and buy the amounts as given. Vary the shades within each color, so that each area changes and shifts subtly as the eye travels over it. For instance, if the principal red is 267, and the auxiliaries are 207 and 210, use two strands of 267 with either one or the other auxiliary most of the time. Sometimes you can tip the balance for a while, and let the auxiliaries predominate. Sometimes you may not mix at all, or use only the auxiliaries. Let your taste be your guide. But keep the overall effect of the area principally that of the main color.

When changing from one shade to another, do so gradually, one strand at a time. For instance, if you wish to go from three strands of the main color to three strands of an auxiliary, first replace one strand of the principal color with the auxiliary. Work a few more rows, replace one more strand of the auxiliary, then complete the transition by replacing the last strand of the principal color with the auxiliary color. Avoid abrupt jumps of value; they will appear as diagonal stripes. When you add a strand, smooth out the yarn so that it lies evenly and the added strand does not stand out from the others.

If you would rather not blend colors, total the amount given for the main and auxiliary colors of each hue, and buy that amount of the main color only. For example, if one pound of 267 (principal) and one-half pound each of 207 and 210 (auxiliaries) are given, just buy two pounds of the principal color (267).

You will find, I think, that as you blend the yarn you will soon fall into the spirit that animates this color mixing, and it will enhance your pleasure in stitching the rug as well as the rug's appearance.

After each color chart there are color notes that indicate how the color effect in the sample was achieved. These suggestions are based on the colors as seen in the original rug. They need not be followed inflexibly, however; adapt them to your own taste, just as variations in the original rugs were made according to the taste of each weaver.

If you are using a yarn other than Persian, instead of separating the strands and mixing simultaneously in the needle, you may mix consecutively. To do this, first stitch with the principal color. Then choose a color that is close in hue to the principal one. Follow with a third color that is slightly different, and then return to the principal color. For this method the auxiliary colors given for Persian yarn may not always be appropriate or available. The colors must be close in hue and tone, otherwise a striped effect will occur. It is best to select blending colors by holding skeins next to each other. Color equivalents for D.M.C. and Bucilla rug yarn are given on page 126.

Note: The color variation in these rugs is such that it is possible to find room for the bits and pieces of yarn you may have left over from other projects. If they are too bright, you can make them fit into the proper color range by dipping them into coffee, tea, or a solution of potassium permanganate (which may be purchased, by prescription, at a drugstore). Mix one tablet of the potassium permanganate in a bowl of warm water. Wet the wool thoroughly first in plain water. Then immerse it in the solution for a short time. The longer you keep it in the solution, the darker it will become. This newly dull color will be permanent. Be careful, because it stains quite readily. It is also possible to change the color of leftover yarn with dye. It is easiest to change any color yarn to brown-black, which can always be used for outlining.

Buying Yarn

It is not necessary to buy all the yarn at once for the projects in this book. The amount of yarn for each color is given, but that amount is necessarily approximate. If you buy the same color at different times there might be a slight variation in the dye lots. Because of the natural color variations in the original rugs, however, consistency is not as crucial as it might be in other needlepoint projects. In fact, inconsistency is an integral part of the originals and should be reflected in the needlepoint in some way. So, if you run short of a color, don't worry. And, if there is wool left over, the remainder may be used for another project from this book, since they use basically the same colors.

The quality of the materials is most important. The materials will become the finished product, and that product and the work you put into it justify using the best materials. Always use natural-fiber yarn made especially for needlepoint or tapestry, *not* yarn made for other purposes, such as knitting yarn, which is too elastic, or crewel yarn, which is too soft (though a single strand of crewel yarn may be used occasionally for blending).

You can save money by buying the yarn by the pound and then cutting it into skeins yourself, as follows: cut the large circular hank at opposite ends. Fold the lengths produced at the center once, so that the cut ends are together. Tie with yarn twice, near the cut and the uncut ends. When you need a thread, pull it from the uncut, folded-over end of the skein.

If yarn of the type needed is unavailable in your area, you can order it by mail (see Mail-Order Sources).

Canvas

In needlepoint, stitches are applied to a piece of canvas to transform it into a heavy textile. The canvas is the foundation. Needlepoint canvas is thick cloth fabric, loosely woven to create holes between the threads. The larger the holes, the fewer stitches per inch the needlepoint will contain. This is indicated by the gauge number of the canvas; for example, #10 canvas has ten threads to the inch. Sizing has been added to the canvas to stiffen it, but the canvas will become more pliable as it is worked.

It is important that the gauge of the canvas be appropriate for the thickness of the yarn. If the yarn is too thin, the canvas will not be completely covered. If it is too thick the mesh will be pulled out of line, and stitching will be difficult.

There are basically two types of needlepoint canvas: mono (single thread) and penelope (double thread). Mono is a hard, twisted cotton thread canvas that comes in many gauges. The kind most suitable for rugs is #10. It is heavy and durable. The size of the holes makes it easy to see for stitching and marking. It is available in 54-inch width, which will accommodate any rug in this book.

A larger-mesh canvas that is suitable is #8 penelope, available in 60-inch width. It is a good quality tan canvas. Because the threads are set in pairs, it is a little more difficult to see the holes.

Both types of canvas cost approximately the same and may be stitched with three strands of Persian yarn. Both should be worked with the selvedge on the edges (sides); the cut ends (top and bottom) should be taped to prevent fraying.

The rugs in this book were designed to fit a single piece of canvas, either #10 mono (fifty-four inches wide) or #8 penelope (sixty inches wide). The canvas dimensions given with each pattern allow for at least a three-inch unworked margin all around the stitched area. If you choose to work on a narrower canvas, you may omit the margins and work right up to the selvedge. Make sure there are enough mesh threads to accommodate the width of the design (the stitch count is given with each pattern). Blocking will be more difficult on a narrower canvas, because you will have to staple or tack into the selvedge, but it still will be possible.

It is far better to work on a single piece of canvas than to join two pieces. The joining process is tedious, especially on a large piece of work such as a rug. But there may be times when it is unavoidable, such as when you wish to make a large rug using #5 canvas or one of the larger rugs on #8 penelope mesh. The #5 mesh is available in a 45-inch and a 60-inch width. Because there are fewer stitches to the inch in this gauge, these widths would not accommodate most rugs in this book. Therefore, the canvas would have to be joined. It is better to join before stitching, preferably on a dividing line of the design, such as that between the field and the border. This will help to conceal the joint. Work this row in cross stitch for added strength.

One way to make a join on penelope or rug canvas is to hold the two pieces face to face with the cut edges to be joined matching. Back stitch a seam between the two threads of the mesh along a row about one inch from the edge. When you turn the canvas to the right side, a two-thread row of the mesh will have been formed at the seam. You can also work this join at the selvedge: fold the right-hand selvedge of one and the left-hand selvedge of the other of the pieces to be joined sharply toward the underside of the canvas. Stitch the seam through the last selvedge warp threads, just where the holes of the canvas start.

Another method of joining, for penelope or rug canvas, is to overlap four rows of the mesh. Work a row of cross stitches down the middle of the overlap with carpet thread. When stitching the overlapped area with yarn, make sure that both pieces are properly aligned, so that the holes match, and work through both layers of canvas.

Additional Supplies

The handcraft of needlework is done today very much as it has been for centuries. The tools are few and modest; no expensive, complicated equipment is necessary. The following items are recommended.

Needles. On #8 canvas, use a #16 needle. On #10 canvas, use either a #16 or #18 (I prefer the larger #16). It's a good idea to have a stock of needles. They do wear out (this is indicated when the shiny surface becomes dull), and a new one works more smoothly. Also, you can thread a number of needles with each of the various colors you are using. When you change colors, you can do so by simply picking up another needle instead of rethreading.

Thimble. I always use one and recommend it to avoid the constant pressure of the needle against your finger. But if you find a thimble awkward or uncomfortable and prefer not to use one, your needlepoint will turn out just as beautiful anyway (I won't vouch for your finger).

Scissors. Good, sharp, pointed embroidery scissors are a necessity to cut the yarn cleanly or lift the stitches if ripping is (regrettably) necessary. To avoid dulling, they should not be used for anything other than embroidery.

Frame. According to your preference, a frame may or may not be used. Though it maintains the shape of the canvas better, it decreases the portability of the work and necessitates a slight adjustment in working methods (that is, working with both hands; one under, one above the canvas). Because of the large size of the

rugs, most conventional needlepoint frames would be too small. You can build a larger frame yourself. Selwyn Cooper, who stitched the Lesghi Star Rug designed and built his own frame on the same principle in which film is loaded in a camera. Using heavy cardboard tubes, he rolled the upper and lower portions of the rug and stitched the section between. You may also use a quilting frame or curtain stretchers.

Marking pens. Be careful in your choice of marking pens for the canvas. To be avoided at all costs are those whose marks will run when wet. Marking pens made especially for canvas are now available, but there are others on the market that are also waterproof and, therefore, safe. To be sure, whatever the label says, test it by making a mark and then wetting that mark. If it does not run, the pen is safe.

Colored pencils. I recommend coloring the graph lightly with the appropriate shade for each area (even when the graph is color keyed). This will help you perceive the design and will make continuous reference to the color photograph unnecessary. The most basic assortment needed consists of red, yellow, blue, black, and white. You can use these to mix any other colors simply by going over one pencil mark with another.

Light. A good light is very important. Daylight, near a window but out of direct sunlight, is best. A good lamp on a movable fixture, such as an adjustable arm or a gooseneck, is also very good. The light should be positioned so that it is shining from above and behind the shoulder opposite the stitching hand.

Basket. This is something I have found to be more than merely a convenience. It is a place where the yarn, cut or uncut, can be kept neatly without getting balled, twisted, or matted, until it is time to be used. The rug itself may be folded and kept there too. A basket is also useful for transporting your project from one room to another.

Masking tape. Other kinds of tape do not stick, or else they leave a residue on the canvas. You need tape to bind the two cut edges of the canvas to keep them from unraveling or catching yarn. The tape should be fairly wide—one and a half or two inches.

Stitching

One of the reasons I enjoy doing needlepoint so much is the actual process of stitching itself. The rhythmic movements of my hand form a cadence that, once established, speeds the work along and lets me concentrate on color and design. I am never out of touch with the piece I am creating; the tactile qualities of wool and canvas and the motions of stitching produce an experience I find comfortable and satisfying.

The stitch that most enhances that feeling for me is the basket-weave stitch. It is a variation, worked on a diagonal, of the basic needlepoint tent stitch, which covers one intersection of the mesh on a slant, from the lower left to the upper right. This stitch allows for a continuous, even, uninterrupted sequence of movements, and, therefore, the work goes very quickly.

Unlike many other needlepoint stitches, the basket weave is accomplished in one motion, so the counting goes easily in a one-to-one ratio with the graph. The canvas is pulled out of shape least when this stitch is used, making the blocking of the finished rug simpler. When done properly, basket-weave stitches lie flat, cover the canvas completely, and have an even, over-all texture. Needlepoint produced using the basket-weave stitch will wear better and last longer because of the thick, woven texture on the back.

The secrets of success with basket weave are to start with enough wool (about a thirty-inch length), to keep the wool untwisted, and always to work each diagonal row in the opposite direction from the one that came before (otherwise a diagonal line will appear on the front). One should work loosely, with an even tension, to ensure that the surface is uniform and the canvas is completely covered. Work with, not against, the weave of the canvas (see figures 1–1 and 1–2). When

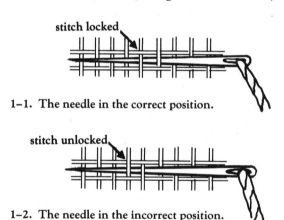

1–1. The needle in the correct position.

1–2. The needle in the incorrect position.

starting and ending, instead of making a knot, simply weave the yarn horizontally or vertically through the completed stitches on the back of the work (not diagonally; this too will show as a line on the front). (Not until the end of the nineteenth century is there evidence of concern for neatness on the underside of an embroidered piece in this country. Until then, a mat of knots and crossed strands was typical. Similarly, some Oriental flat woven rugs have secondary weft threads floating on the back. The extra thicknesses of wool function as a padding that increases the life of the textile. You might consider this practice in your own work.)

Use the basket-weave stitch as often as possible, except when making a single row, such as an outline, or when filling in small or oddly shaped areas, where it would be impractical. Because of the weave on the back, the basket weave uses the greatest amount of yarn, but the finished product looks, wears, and handles best of any needlepoint made with the tent stitch. (The tent stitch and no other needlepoint stitch should be used because the surface of these rugs should be flat and even.) Stitches that cover more than one intersection of the canvas or protrude from the surface will not look or wear well. The decorative qualities of these rug designs come from the outlines and colors, not from the stitching, which should simply show the design plainly.

The Basket-Weave Stitch

The basket-weave stitch is made by stitching adjacent diagonal rows, working up one row, then down the row directly to the left, then up the row to the left of that, and so on (figures 1–3 through 1–14). Each new row is always worked to the left of the previous one. The stitches of each subsequent row interlock with those of the previous row.

As you can see in the series of photographs, the needle is held in a horizontal position when working in a diagonal row up the canvas and in a vertical position when working down the canvas. The only exception is the last stitch of each diagonal row, for which the needle is held in a diagonal position in order to emerge in the proper place for the first stitch of the next row.

Adapting a Design

An Oriental rug is designed to be used just as it comes off the loom. It is a single unit: nothing needs to be added to it; it is not intended to be cut or reshaped like a piece of cloth. Since it is usually meant to go on the floor, it is designed to be looked at from all angles. It is always symmetrical in some way.

The two basic parts of an Oriental rug design are the *field* and the *border* that frames the field. The border will often have colors that are not in the field but support and complement it. Often the main border is flanked by two narrow-band borders called *guard stripes* or *guard bands*. Border designs are always repeating patterns. The relationship of border to field may be likened to a window through which one views a part of an infinite world.

Though it is always the focus of the design, there is a wide range of ways in which the field may be handled. For instance, using examples from this book, it may:

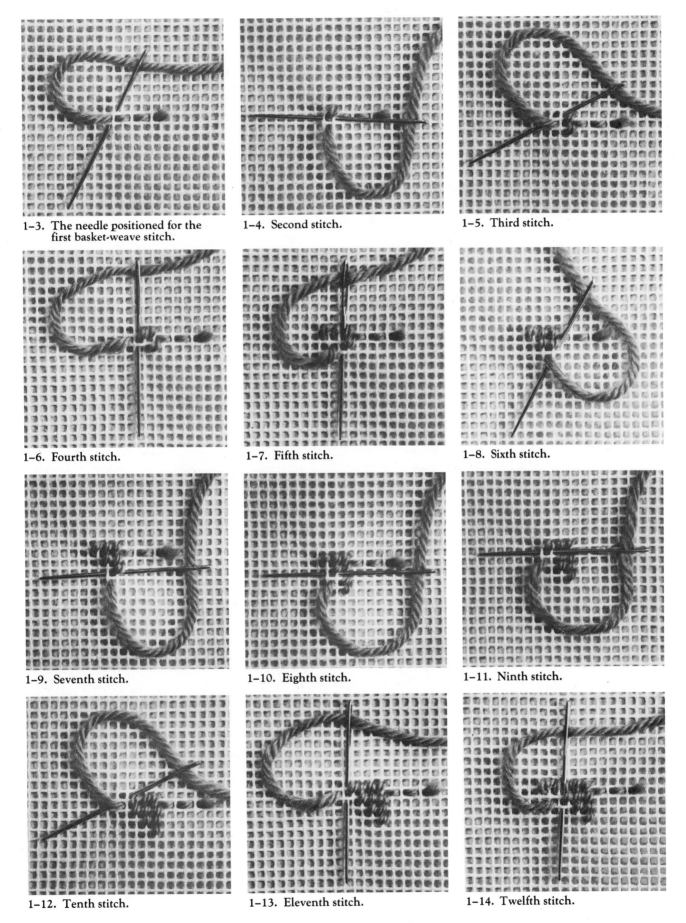

1–3. The needle positioned for the first basket-weave stitch.

1–4. Second stitch.

1–5. Third stitch.

1–6. Fourth stitch.

1–7. Fifth stitch.

1–8. Sixth stitch.

1–9. Seventh stitch.

1–10. Eighth stitch.

1–11. Ninth stitch.

1–12. Tenth stitch.

1–13. Eleventh stitch.

1–14. Twelfth stitch.

15

- have one large central medallion (see Turkish Mat)
- have two or three medallions (see Bergama Rug or Lesghi Star Rug)
- consist of repeating medallions (see Caucasian Rug)
- have many field designs made up of an all-over pattern (see Shirvan Rug)

Each has its own structural principles, which will serve as a guide in perceiving the design. For example, in the designs with central medallions the center lines are important since they are the axes around which the designs are constructed. In the designs with two or three medallions, the fact that the design is divided into upper and lower halves is very important, since both halves are the same. In repeating medallion designs, the dividing lines are significant since they enclose equal rectangles within which the medallions are symmetrically placed. In all-over patterns, the principle of the repeat and the distribution of the motifs is of prime importance.

The list could go on, for the vein of visual invention that went into the designing of Oriental rugs was extremely rich. These are but a few among many design techniques. Even within the categories, each rug is unique. An awareness of the principle that applies to the design will help in adapting it to another size or purpose.

A technique for making a smaller rug using the same designs is to reduce the size of the field, keeping the scale of the motifs the same. This principle is most often used with repeating patterns. (It is explored, using the Lotto Rug, in figures 3-12, 3-13, and 3-14.) For example, there are fifteen rectangular motifs in the field of the Caucasian Rug (three horizontally by five vertically). A smaller adaptation might be made by using only six motifs (two horizontally by three vertically). For a larger rug, the size of the field and the number of motifs would be increased. If the size of the field were changed, the length of the border and, possibly, the turnings at the corners would have to be adjusted. Border patterns are designed to turn in a visually pleasing way. To plan a new turning, you may hold a mirror upright and at a 45-degree angle standing on the border pattern. The drawing plus the reflection will make an **L** and will show how the turning may be accomplished.

Another way of adapting rug designs for use in smaller pieces has come not from the Orient but from the West. Often a wornout carpet had unworn portions that were too handsome to be thrown away. The unworn portions were made into upholstery, bags, or other small items. These appear from time to time at auction or in antique shops that specialize in textiles.

A part of a rug design could be used as a pillow or chair seat. Like Greek or Roman sculpture, a fragment suggests the whole and may even be charming simply because it *is* fragmentary. One can make use of this idea in a number of ways. A wide border design could be used alone, as a bag with a flap. For instance, using the Shirvan Rug border one panel could be used for the front, one for the back, and one for the flap. (I have actually seen one like this in an antique shop.) A medallion design, such as one of the two large octagons of the Bergama Rug, could be used singly for a cushion. In fact, an entire rug could be stuffed and used as a very large cushion. This would be similar to one of the original uses of these rugs: they were sometimes stuffed with dried beans and people sat upon them on the floor or ground. You can also simply use a random fragment, not necessarily symmetrical, possibly containing part of both the border and the field. It is surprising to see how attractive just about any segment of an Oriental rug can be (I have noticed this when photographing details. It is just about impossible to take a bad-looking photograph, unless it simply does not come out).

Smaller projects can be an introduction to these designs or a way of using up left-over yarn after stitching a rug. A good way to plan a small project is to cut a small square or rectangle of the desired proportions out of a sheet of paper, then place it over the color plate. As you move this "mask" over the surface, many attractive designs will appear—simply select the one you like best.

You may create coordinate patterns to use as accessories to go with your rug. Design ideas for projects of this kind are given with each rug. Pillow and upholstery designs may use the pattern in new ways and be placed in the same room as the rug to create a striking effect. For example, in the Shirvan Rug, use a single motif, or a few motifs, from the field, expand the pattern of the guard bands to make an all-over repeat, or use it as a stripe pattern; in the border pattern the motifs may be employed as repeating medallions. Color changes can also be effective. For instance, try stitching the floral motifs in dark colors on a light ground.

You may also interchange borders. I have seen a beautiful Lotto rug bordered by cloud band motifs, such as those in the Rug with Spots and Stripes.

As well as making them more useful, adapting these rug designs to other uses will increase your appreciation of the artistry of the original designers. To plan a new design, sketch the motifs using tracing paper over the color plate and plot the design on graph paper.

2. TRANSFERRING THE DESIGN

The Graph

On early charts used for knotted rugs of complex design the lines were laboriously hand ruled; graph paper did not exist. Such charts were needed particularly for curvilinear designs, which had to be carefully and accurately plotted. These drawings are called *cartoons*, which, in this instance, means "model." In the first development of these cartoons, pinholes designated the outline of the design. Later, outlines were made in ink or pencil, and the shapes were filled in with colors.

These charts were produced by skilled designers, draftsmen, and colorists for town factories where the amount of use they were put to could repay the time and trouble that went into their making. In some factories where many weavers were employed, one person would call out the knot count from the chart and each weaver would follow on her loom. Tribal or village weavers almost never used cartoons; they memorized the knot count or worked from the back of an existing carpet.

A tribal or village rug is usually a straight-line design that may be woven directly on the loom. Although most of the rugs in this book were probably made without the use of a complete cartoon, a graph can be an invaluable tool for the modern needlepointer. These angular designs respect the warp and weft of the weaving medium and, therefore, easily follow the horizontal, vertical, and diagonal of the graph paper and the needlepoint canvas. The stitch count of each line of these designs is clearly shown on the graph. These counts usually repeat, so that once you have stitched a particular count a few times, further reference to the graph may be unnecessary. Once the pattern is established, the stitching flows easily, but the graph is there to refresh your memory.

When using a graph for needlepoint, you start with a blank canvas. The design exists only as a notation on the graph, just as music exists only as notes on music paper before it is played. You put the design on the canvas by referring to this notation. The proper position of each stitch on an intersection of the threads of the canvas is clearly shown on the squared paper. Each box of the graph stands for one needlepoint stitch. The graph is a detailed diagram of the design, *not* a picture of the unworked canvas. You can find the number of stitches in any given line by counting the number of graph boxes. When you are using the tent stitch, each box on an unworked canvas corresponds to one intersection of the warp and weft.

In the patterns in this book the outline is drawn in black, giving a clear picture of the design. Using colored pencils, you may fill in the shapes lightly to get a good idea of what a colored cartoon might have looked like.

Seeing how these designs are put together and how the parts connect and interact can be your greatest aid to working. Even before picking up your marker or needle, the first step should be simply to look at the design, to see the basic construction, the major lines and the important shapes. Before your hand takes over, try to make the design reveal its logic to your eye. These designs are orderly and logical, adhering to simple rules of symmetry and repetition. One key to seeing a design clearly can be the sequence in which you think of working it. Suggestions are given with each pattern for the sequence in which it should be marked and stitched. These are based upon my experience in charting the designs.

If you have never worked from a graph before, it might be a good idea to practice on a small piece of canvas first, stitching a motif or a portion of a design. One practice piece should be more than adequate to accustom you to translating the graph boxes into stitches. Then, working on the actual rug, you will find the simple mechanics of the process become second nature (one graph box equals one stitch).

Preparing the Canvas

To begin, you will need a canvas of the proper size, a work table, masking tape, and two marking pens. The work surface should be large enough so that you can lay all or most of the canvas on it. Sheets of white paper or white cloth placed on the table top will make the canvas threads easier to see and will protect the table's surface from the waterproof marking pens. One pen should be of medium tone (to reproduce the heavy lines of the graph on the canvas) and the other should be dark (to mark the outlines of the design).

First tape the two cut ends of the canvas so that they will not unravel or catch the yarn when you are stitching. Place the tape along the end of the canvas so that you can fold it over lengthwise. Mark one taped end as top.

Mark the center of the canvas. You can find that

point by folding the canvas horizontally in half and vertically in half.

Note: The canvas threads will be easier to see if your light source does not produce strong shadows from the canvas.

Transferring the Design

There are four steps in transferring the design to the canvas. First, reproduce every tenth (heavy) line of the graph paper on the canvas, thereby creating a grid of squares of one hundred stitches. Second, draw the dividing lines of the border. Third, draw the outlines of the motifs. Finally, fill in with various colored yarns.

Step One: Reproducing the Graph Lines. After the canvas ends have been taped, place the canvas flat on your work table. Uncurl it by rolling it once or twice in the opposite direction from the way it curls. Fold the canvas in half again to find center, and mark the center.

Counting will be easier if you reproduce on your canvas the heavy lines that appear every tenth line on

the graph. Use the medium-tone marker (e.g., blue or tan). Start at the center and draw these lines *between* the threads of the canvas. Although counting and marking these lines can be done simultaneously, I prefer to count first with the point of a pin. Count ten threads and stick the point of the pin into the tenth thread. Check the count. If it is correct, draw a short line between the tenth and eleventh mesh thread. Extend these lines to form squares of one hundred stitches each, just as the large squares of the graph contain one hundred small boxes (figures 2–1 and 2–2).

Step Two: Drawing the Dividing Lines of the Borders. Here you begin to draw the design. Using the same color marker you used to draw the graph lines, mark the horizontal and vertical center threads of the canvas. Make sure you draw *on* the threads of the canvas. Extend these lines to divide the canvas into quarters. These are the center lines of your design. They appear in the same position on the graph in all the designs in this book (figures 2–3 and 2–4). From the center count the appropriate number of graph boxes and mark the outer edge of the design. The

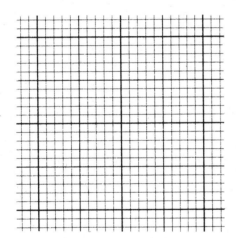

2–1. A detail of the graph with ten by ten boxes indicated by a heavy line.

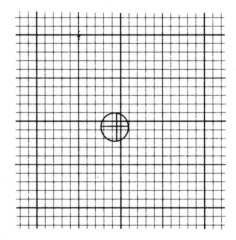

2–3. The center mark on the graph.

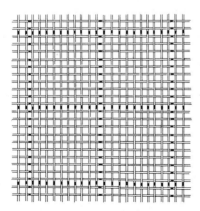

2–2. The ten by ten boxes reproduced on the canvas.

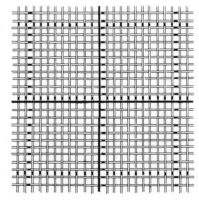

2–4. The center lines marked on the canvas.

18

graph-thread count is given for each design. All the rugs are designed with an odd number of stitches. When divided in half, the center thread will be left over. There will always be an equal number of threads and graph boxes on either side of the center. For example, if the horizontal graph-thread count is 201, there will be 100 threads (boxes) to the right, and 100 threads (boxes) to the left of the center. Because I have found that knowing the number of threads on either side of the center makes marking the outer edge easier, I have given these figures for each rug. To find these numbers I subtracted one from the total graph-thread count both horizontally and vertically and divided by two. For example, in the Shirvan Rug the graph thread count is 365 by 549. Horizontally, there are 182 stitches on either side of the center thread (182 plus 182 plus one equals 365). Vertically, there are 274 stitches on either side of the center thread (274 plus 274 plus one equals 549).

Draw the dividing lines of the borders *on* the threads of the canvas. This will become a stitched line. Use a marker the same color as the stitches. After drawing the outer edge of the design, draw the remaining dividing lines of the border. Use the table given with each design. To make sure your counting is correct, check the total number of stitches by counting along the diagonal at the corners.

Step Three: Drawing the Design. This is where the motifs of the design are outlined on the canvas and begin to form the pattern. The outline is a very important aspect in the design of an Oriental rug. Nearly all the motifs are outlined, most in brown-black and some in a contrasting color. This line between areas brings the colors vibrantly to life, delineates the patterns sharply, and helps to place the design.

The proper placement of the outlines of the design depends on correct counting of the motifs and the spaces between them. Each rug will develop differently, according to the requirements of its design. I prefer to begin marking in the center of the design, because the canvas will then be easier to handle when you begin stitching. As you work from the center, slide the rug up or down on the table and let it hang off the edge. When stitching, roll the sides inward so that you can grasp the canvas. When you have a large enough area outlined, begin to fill in with colored yarn (Step Four). I usually work the lower half of the design first, then turn it around to work the upper half.

Working suggestions are given with each pattern, but if you have a different approach with which you feel more comfortable, by all means use it.

Step Four: Filling in the Design. This is where the outlines are filled in and the design becomes a rug. You will see the design emerge through the steady flow of the stitching, with first one color and then another bringing to the pattern its visual delight. Like tasting a dish while it is cooking, this step is the source of much of the joy of making rugs.

Working Tips

When you have finished stitching for the day, it is a good idea to press or steam the work to make blocking easier and to keep the canvas in shape. Place it face down and pull gently in the opposite direction from that in which it is leaning. Hold a steamer or a steam iron about two inches from the work and steam the canvas, or press on the wrong side; do not iron the stitches flat. While steaming or pressing, tug gently to straighten the needlepoint.

Stitching the outline sometimes requires maneuvering. I often switch from my right hand to my left, or simply place single stitches from the front to the back of the canvas. Technique does not matter as much with outlining as with the fill-in stitches. The main concern is that the stitches are in the right position on the canvas. All stitches should be slanting from the lower left to the upper right of the intersections of the threads. Outlining requires concentration, so try to do it when you are relaxed and feel able to give the work your full attention. Filling in is pure pleasure.

Keep many needles threaded with different colors within easy reach. You will then be able to work continuously for extended periods without stopping to rethread.

At least one extra row of stitches is required beyond the outermost line given on the graph. It is into this row (or rows) that the binding stitches are worked. Instructions with each pattern provide information on the stitching of extra rows.

3. THE RUGS

The Oriental Rug

Of all the textile arts in the world, Oriental rugs must be considered among the most beautiful; not only are they decorative objects, but they were an integral part of the lives of the people who made them and the deepest expression of their creativity.

What we call an Oriental rug is a heavy textile that is hand woven on a loom. The warp threads are stretched vertically, and the weft threads are passed horizontally in and out of these. In pile rugs short pieces of wool are knotted around the warp threads. At the end of each row weft threads are run between the rows to hold the knots in position (figure 3–1).

3–1. Symmetrical knot or Turkish knot. In pile rugs short pieces of wool are knotted around the warp threads. The loose ends of the knots form the pile.

Portability was a priority to the original rugmakers, who carried their belongings with them from place to place. Everything about a rug and its manufacture meets the portability requirement, starting with the source of the wool. The sheep were driven from one grazing ground to another. In their travels with their herds, people gathered plants and other raw materials that were used to dye the wool. For this purpose they sometimes had a traveling "filing cabinet," a jacket with many pockets, one for each color. The loom upon which the rug was woven was portable, too, being merely a frame that could easily be dismantled and reassembled. The rug itself could simply be rolled up whenever it was time to move on.

Rugs were a necessity; each rug filled one of many possible uses. It could be used as a ground cover (important as this is in a tent), or as a bed cover, cradle, saddle cover, door, cushion, luggage—among other uses. To us, looking at such rugs in a different time and place, they represent one of the wonderful mysteries of the human spirit. We can trace and understand their practical uses, but the extraordinary effort and skill necessary to make them beautiful reaches far deeper,

and we respond to it immediately. The weavers could have made countless undyed and undesigned rugs more easily. Instead, they made marvelous creations that were more than practical: they were life enriching, reflecting the traditions of a culture and the intuitions of the weaver.

In this nomadic society, the rug was a central part of life. Looms, their rugs in all stages before completion, were ever present. Women were always working at the looms or at spinning yarn. Men tended and sheared the sheep and dyed the wool. At an early age children were taught to take their place in the process. Through the seasons and migrations, the accumulation of the rugmakers' labor could be seen near the doorways of their dwelling places, the rugs gradually but persistently, row by row, nearing completion.

A very important historical factor in the development of rugs was the rise and spread of Islam. The earliest Islamic carpets known were found in this century in mosques in the Turkish towns of Konya and Bey Shehir; these carpets date to the thirteenth and fourteenth centuries. As the nomads converted to Islam, other Islamic peoples began to use woven rugs, which became an indication of wealth and were even placed beneath the feet of royalty. The rugs' form also changed, reflecting their new roles. They pervaded every level of society, rich and poor, the countryside, villages, and cities. The nomads and villagers made them for their own use; they were made in manufactories for the sultans and mosques; and they were made in the villages and cities as items of commerce.

In his travels in the thirteenth century Marco Polo called the Oriental carpets he saw the most beautiful in the world. By the fifteenth century, significant numbers were being exported to Europe through Venice. Rugs were highly valued and were displayed in honored places in churches and wealthy homes throughout Europe. They were depicted in paintings, sometimes so frequently by an individual artist that his name became associated with a particular type of rug. After a hiatus, trading of Oriental rugs resurged in the nineteenth century in the West; this activity culminated in the great collections amassed in this century. One such is that of Joseph V. McMullen, now in the Metropolitan Museum of Art, from which five rugs have been adapted for this book.

The rugs selected for adaptation here are either Turkish or Caucasian. Of all the handmade Oriental rugs, these are among the best suited for the kind of needlepoint we do today. The scale of the knots is quite similar to commonly used needlepoint canvas. The designs represent a wide range of expression, but they share an angular, graphic quality, with bold color combinations, to which the modern sensibility responds. Because they fit well into the geometry of the canvas, these designs are readily graphed for and worked in needlepoint.

The rugs in this book are classics of their types, some of the finest examples from a long history of rugmaking. They epitomize the weaver's art and grow out of the medium in a way particularly their own, incorporating the influences of other decorative arts. In many cases they were designed by the weavers themselves. For these reasons I think you will find these designs particularly congenial for interpretation in needlepoint. As you work, it will surely become more and more clear why these rug designs were treasured by so many different people and why they have outlived fashions, generations, and empires.

Handwork

The great painter Pierre-Auguste Renoir had a job in his youth painting decorations on china plates. But, as his son, Jean Renoir, relates, he lost it when a machine was invented that could do the job. It was not so much that the machine was faster; the workers in the factory managed to match its production by organizing themselves efficiently and working at top speed. But the plates made by the machine were all the same, and this was exactly what people wanted in the era when the marvels of industrialization first appeared. The hand-painters could not match this uniformity, and so the factory closed down. If one could authenticate a plate as having been painted by the young Renoir, with all its "imperfections," it would be highly valued today.

By great effort it is possible for a person to match the near-precision of a machine. But it is not desirable. All that is accomplished is to squeeze every trace of humanity and personality out of the finished product. We are forced by industrialization to accept machine-made products—those made by hand would be far too expensive—and their uniformity has crept into our ideal of beauty. People sometimes think of imperfections and irregularities that characterize handwork as mistakes, but they are not. There is something in handwork that we recognize as reflecting the spirit, heart, and mind of the person who made it.

The originals from which the rugs in this book were adapted were made by hand in a preindustrial society on a kind of loom that has existed for centuries. The "imperfections" we see are irregular drawing, colors that vary and repeat at random, corner turnings of the border that may be awkward and unmatched, and,

sometimes, a field design that is cut off arbitrarily. These qualities do not mar the design, they simply show us the hand of the weaver. The rugs contain a marvelous sense of life. The graphs of the rugs that are presented in this book are necessarily drawn more regularly than the originals, but I encouraged those who stitched the samples to be free in their color interpretations, to love their "mistakes," and to let their own hand lead them into the spirit of the rugs.

As you work from the illustrations in this book, let them be your servants and guides but not your masters. The graphs are intended to be a record of the design, just as music notation is a record of a piece of music but is not the music itself. Like a musician in performance, the needleworker's interpretation and spontaneity distinguish a piece of work. The original weavers of the rugs did not attempt to copy a previous model perfectly, yet we consider what they made to be just right. Improvisation and constant reinterpretation rather than slavish, machinelike precision will not only create a more beautiful product but will greatly enhance your pleasure in the process.

This does not mean that there are no rules, or that anything is permissible. There is structure to an Oriental rug, just as there is structure to music or any art form. Even a great innovator like Beethoven worked within tradition, transforming it but also preserving it. The rug patterns that follow were adapted from originals in the collections listed in the Appendix. Adaptations vary in their closeness to the originals; some are freely interpreted, others more carefully plotted. In all instances, however, the adaptations are identified with the names of the original pile rugs.

The suggestions and patterns that follow will, I hope, show you how Oriental rugs were created. Even more, I hope that this understanding will allow you to embark with confidence on your project, which is as much an adventure as the rug itself is a special treasure to keep.

Rugs from the Caucasus

In doing research for this book I conjured up exotic images in my mind of the places where these rugs were made. These images persisted despite evidence to the contrary. To me, the "Caucasus" and the "shores of the Black Sea" were as shrouded in mystery as the name of the sea itself. Therefore, I was surprised, upon attending a lecture that included slides made from photographs of the region taken in the late nineteenth century, to see that the reality was quite different from what I had imagined, although possibly more intriguing.

Rather than pictures only of nomads wandering the

lonely mountain ranges, there were also urban industrial environments, with smokestacks, factories, and rows of blocklike buildings. The downtowns were complete with boulevards, parks, and, in one instance, a Victorian opera house. Although the pastoral setting in which the rugs were originally developed existed side by side with the cities, many of the rugs of the late nineteenth century were made commercially in towns in the same way as ever—by hand.

The four rug designs that follow are from the region between the Black Sea (on the west) and the Caspian Sea (on the east), which includes the Greater and Lesser Caucasian mountain ranges. A potpourri of nationalities, languages, and ways of life coexist there: Turks, Georgians, Armenians, Persians, Kurds, Slavs—about 350 different tribes, including nomads, villagers, and city dwellers, speaking approximately 150 different dialects. Today most of this area is part of the Soviet Union.

Rugs from the Caucasus were not well known in the West until this century because there wasn't much commerce to and from that isolated region. In fact, we know of no Caucasian pile-woven rug that predates the seventeenth century (it may be assumed that those rugs existed but simply did not survive). Many of the rugs that are available to us are relatively recent, dating from the late nineteenth or early twentieth centuries. By that time rug knotting had become such an important industry in the region that for some districts it was the chief source of revenue, engaging more than half the population. In the 1920s, the Soviet government encouraged rug weaving for export to raise badly needed foreign capital.

As Caucasian rugs have become known to Westerners, they have impressed connoisseurs and collectors with their simplicity and beauty. The strong color combinations and monumental scale of designs seem to parallel aspects of modern abstract paintings. Perhaps this is a reason for the rugs' current popularity. Good Caucasian rugs are highly sought after today. The best examples are usually to be found in museum collections.

Caucasian rugs are usually identified by the localities from which they come, though this can be complicated by cross-influence and intermarriage. These rugs rarely exceed six by nine feet (30 cm by 270 cm), especially those of the eighteenth and nineteenth centuries. The reason for their relatively small size is that the Caucasus, a comparatively poor region, did not have opulent palaces and mansions as did Persia and Turkey. Caucasian rugs were originally made on small looms for local use. Only later was it discovered how desirable they would become to the rest of the world.

SHIRVAN RUG

46" by 68½" (117 cm × 174 cm) on #8 penelope canvas

The original rug comes from the Shirvan region on the coastal plain of the southwest Caucasus near the Caspian Sea, an area of prolific rug production in the nineteenth century. Because they were woven on narrow looms, many rugs from there had a characteristic long, thin shape. In this adaptation, the rug was shortened and the coloring of the field made somewhat more uniform, variations I thought suitable for modern use.

This rug combines a colorful over-all floral pattern in the field with a stately border. The geometric floral motifs of the field are arranged in diagonal rows on a dark blue ground. Small white buds between the flowers add a magical, starry quality—I think of a garden under the night sky. Each flower contains a star motif within a diamond shape. Little animals adorn the bottom of the field.

The border is among the most beautiful found in Caucasian rugs. It is made up of interlaced forms derived from the angular Kufic script, an archaic kind of Arabic lettering often used in the decorative arts. This alternates with medallions with curling outlines, which makes a nice contrast. In the whole design the blue ground is used as a foil for the brightly colored flowers outlined in various colors in the field and the white linear forms of the border.

Color

	Principal Colors (10)		Auxiliary Colors (4)	
Color	Amount	Paternayan Yarn No.	Amount	Paternayan Yarn No.
dark brown	1 lb.	112		
ivory	¾ lb.	136		
dark blue	1¼ lbs.	321	3 oz.	365
			1 oz.	305
red	½ lb.	267		
gold	¾ lb.	433	10 strands	145
light blue	¼ lb.	380	20 strands	342
pink	2 oz.	234		
olive	1 oz.	583		
yellow	1 oz.	445		
light brown	2 oz.	104		

Pink appears in some of the floral motifs. It creates a lively color effect, but it might originally have been a red that has faded. In similar versions of this rug, no pink appears. You may substitute red if you wish.

If you want a crisper, more graphic design, you may omit the auxiliary shades and use only the main colors, but mixing the shades with the main colors gives this rug an authentic look.

For background field, mix 321 with 365. Use 321 and 305 for the background border.

To get the mixed light blue color in the motifs, combine 380 with 342. You may use 380 all by itself, but not 342, because it is too bright.

Do not use mixed colors of yarn for outlining.

Directions

1. Prepare a piece of #8 penelope canvas 52" by 72" (124.5 cm by 182.9 cm).

2. Mark the corresponding (heavy) graph lines.

3. Mark the center horizontal and vertical threads of the canvas.

4. Mark the outer edge of the design. The graph thread count is 365 by 549. Horizontally, there are 182 stitches on either side of the center thread. Vertically, there are 274 stitches on either side of the center thread.

5. Mark the dividing lines of the border. Start from the outer edge, using the following table.

Outer edge	**1 stitch**
Barber's pole band	2 stitches
Dividing line	**1 stitch**
Guard band	12 stitches
Dividing line	**1 stitch**
Barber's pole band	2 stitches
Dividing line	**1 stitch**
Kufic border	49 stitches
Dividing line	**1 stitch**
Barber's pole band	2 stitches
Dividing line	**1 stitch**
Guard band	12 stitches
Dividing line	**1 stitch**
Barber's pole band	2 stitches
Dividing line (field line)	**1 stitch**
Total width of border =	89 stitches

6. Outline the floral motifs in the field. The colors of the outlines vary along diagonal rows, one row being all red and the other alternately blue and gold. Use corresponding colored markers or stitch directly onto the canvas.

7. Outline the diamond and star motifs. Continue marking and stitching the outlines of the motifs. Put in the small white squares.

8. When you have outlined about five motifs, fill in the shapes and the background with colored yarn. (Or you may choose to do all the outlining first and fill in later.)

9. Begin working the narrow guard band at the lower right. Stitch the small motifs and triangles with dark brown, 112. Stitch the red squares. Fill in the remainder of the pattern with gold 433. Note that one motif at each corner will have an extra stitch because this border was designed with an even number of stitches, while the rest of the rug has an odd number of stitches.

10. Work the main border. Outline the motifs with red marker, or stitch directly onto the canvas. Follow the stitch count indicated on the graphs. The stem of the **Y** at either side of the rosette is sometimes four, and sometimes five stitches. This was done to fit the border into the available space. Also note the slight difference between the drawing of the hooks in the side borders and those in the top and bottom borders.

11. When the outline is complete, fill in the design with colored yarn, using Color Plate C–1 and the color code as a guide.

12. For this rug no extra rows of stitches are required. Work the binding directly into the outermost row of the design.

Design Ideas for Coordinate Patterns

Use one or more of the floral motifs of the field for an individual piece.

Create a geometric pattern of adjacent rows of the guard band. You may include the barber's pole band to form a striped pattern.

Make an all-over pattern using the Kufic motif and medallions of the main border.

Repeat the star and diamond at the center of each floral motif for a patchwork-like design.

■	dark brown
□	ivory
⊡	red
⊠	blue
◩	gold

CAUCASIAN RUG 40″ by 55″ (102 cm × 140 cm) on #8 penelope canvas

The organizing principle of design in this rug—the continuous rectangle pattern further elaborated by octagons and diamonds—resembles tiles fitted together and may have been an attempt to imitate (in woven, portable floor coverings) the great mosaic floors of palaces. Although the rug from which this is adapted was made in the Caucasus in the late nineteenth century, this pattern has been in use in Turkish rug weaving since the 1400s. The principle is a simple one. The motif, here repeated fifteen times, may be used as many or as few times as desired to fill a given area, just as though you were fitting a floor with tiles.

In this design the red octagons within the rectangles are hung with latch hooks that "catch" the eye. These are the focus of a positive-negative interplay: are they dark hooks on a light ground, or light hooks on a dark ground? Are the red octagons themselves the background to an interlace of white diamonds, or are they sitting on a white ground? This is a fascinating element present in many Oriental rug designs.

Within the octagons are motifs with hooks jutting from every corner and side. Horizontal rows 2, 3, and 4 of these are drawn the same. Rows 1 and 5 are the same but the top row omits the small triangle at either side. The narrow border of zigzags and diamonds frames the design simply, in keeping with its character. Note the white triangle along the border (right side of rug). Such a singular element differing from the overall coloring is to remind us of the "imperfection of all things."

Most Oriental rugs were finished with a band of flat weave at each end. These are often missing from old rugs because they do not wear well. In the original rug of this design, the ends have remained and seem an integral part of the design, like a porch that is an important part of a house even though it is not structurally necessary. Therefore, I designed rows of soumak (knit) stitching, worked with a single strand of Persian yarn at either end, to re-create this expansive feeling.

To vary the field, 267, a brownish red, is mixed with 210, a pinkish red. Should you prefer a softer quality, invert the amounts given.

The green in Oriental rugs is rarely a consistent color. To create a varied effect, mix 512 with 516. If you wish to use only one color, choose either 512 or 516.

Although colors of the small squares of the border appear in a regular pattern in this adaptation, those in the original rug do not. You might choose to work the border in a random color arrangement.

Directions

1. Prepare a piece of #8 penelope canvas 46″ by 61″ (117 cm by 155 cm).

2. Mark the corresponding (heavy) graph lines.

3. Mark the center horizontal and vertical threads of the canvas.

4. Mark the outer edge of the design. The graph thread count is 343 by 419. Horizontally, there are 171 stitches on either side of the center thread. Vertically, there are 209 stitches on either side of the center thread.

5. Mark the dividing lines of the border. Start from the outer edge, using the following table.

Outer edge	**1 stitch**
Band of squares	3 stitches
Dividing line	**1 stitch**
Band of diamonds	9 stitches
Dividing line	**1 stitch**
Band of squares	3 stitches
Dividing line	**1 stitch**
Zigzag band	9 stitches
Dividing line (field line)	**1 stitch**
Total width of border =	30 stitches

6. Put in the fifteen rectangular panels. Draw the diagonal lines at the corners to form the octagons.

7. When this is done, continue marking the "hooks" on the sides of the octagon. Mark the adjacent blue or green line.

8. Place the center crosses in each of the fifteen motifs. Lightly tint the graph with colored pencils. This will make the pattern easier to count and stitch. Outline the motifs.

9. Use a cross-stitch for the single gold or ivory stitch within the motifs to create a stronger accent.

10. Work the striped bands between the panels, following the color code on the graph.

11. Fill in the remainder of the field with colored yarns using Color Plate C–2 as a guide.

Color

	Principal Colors (6)		Auxiliary Colors (4)	
Color	Amount	Paternayan Yarn No.	Amount	Paternayan Yarn No.
dark brown	$\frac{1}{2}$ lb.	**112**	$\frac{1}{2}$ lb.	114
ivory	$\frac{3}{4}$ lb.	**136**		
red	$1\frac{1}{4}$ lbs.	**267**	$\frac{1}{2}$ lb.	210
blue	$\frac{1}{2}$ lb.	**323**	$\frac{1}{4}$ lb.	311
gold	$\frac{1}{2}$ lb.	**433**		
green	$\frac{1}{4}$ lb.	**512**	$\frac{1}{4}$ lb.	516

12. Work the zigzag and narrow geometric borders.

13. Stitch an extra row of red on either edge of the rug. Work the binding stitch into this row, using the same color yarn.

Soumak Border

To do the soumak stitch (figure 3–2) turn the canvas ninety degrees. Work with the selvedges facing you. Work each single stitch from hole one to two to three, back to one, and then to four. Continue down in the direction shown. Work all rows from the upper to the lower selvedge, and end off and begin a new thread for each row. Stitches in adjacent rows will share the same holes at the tops of the two prongs of the V. Half stitches are used to fill in the empty spaces at the ends of the rows.

Design Ideas for Coordinate Patterns

Use a single rectangular panel, with or without a border, as an individual piece.

Place the zigzag bands next to each other to form a pattern of alternately colored chevrons.

The squares or diamonds of the border bands could be employed in an all-over pattern.

For a simple stripe pattern, repeat the Soumak border.

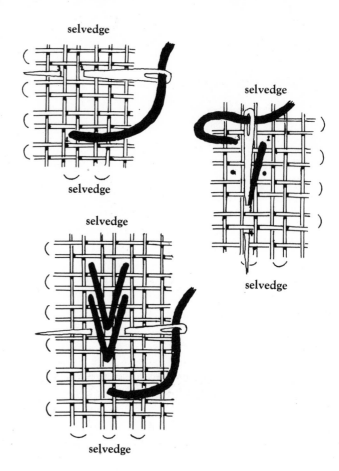

3–2. Working the Soumak stitch in different directions.

| | dark brown |
| | red |

34

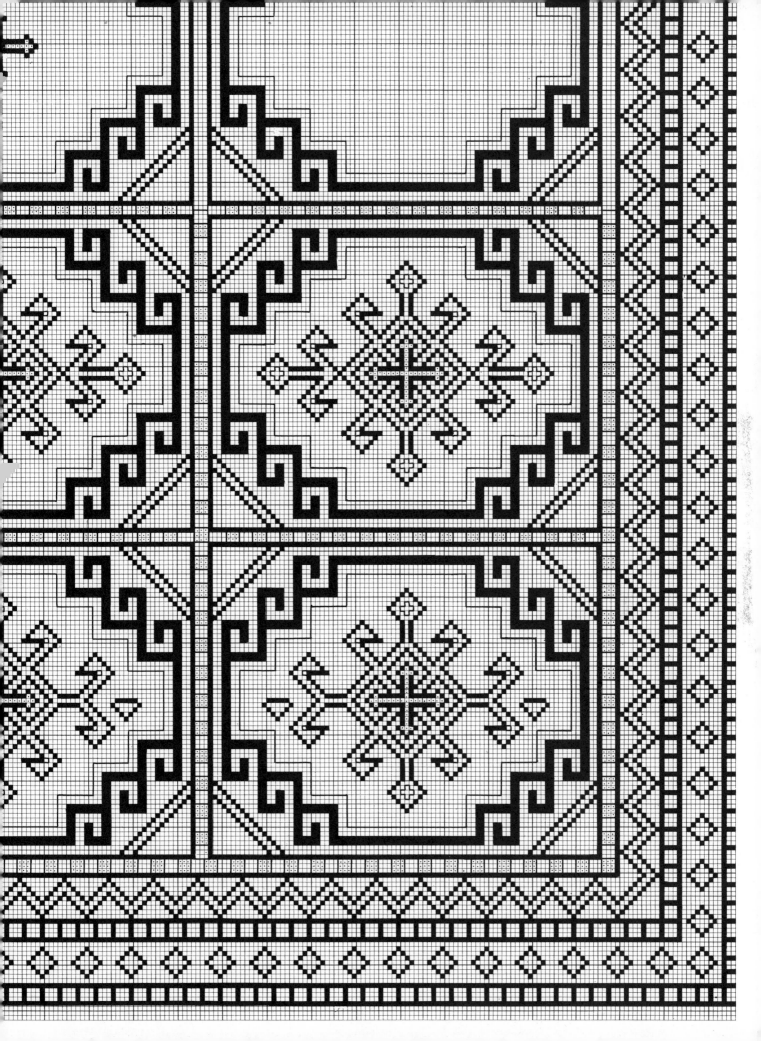

GEOMETRICAL KAZAK

48″ by 60″ (122 cm × 152 cm) on #10 mono canvas

Kazak rugs were made by the country people of the valleys and plateaus of the southwest Caucasus mountains, where Persia, Turkey, and the Caucasian region come together. A relatively limited number of designs are known to us, but they are distinctive and often easy to identify by their characteristic rich color, graphic design, and long pile (as high as three-quarters of an inch). The bold quality of these designs is a likely consequence of the high pile (which might blur or obscure the detail of an intricate design); the pile intensifies the richness of the color, which can be seen at both surface and depth..

Kazak rug production reached its peak before the turn of the century, after the region was conquered by Russia. By the early 1900s production was declining because of a breakdown in traditions of the craft, such as the introduction of chemical dyes.

The original from which this rug was adapted is an example of a popular Kazak design. In the field the central rectangular medallion is flanked by a panel of secondary elements in each corner. This is called a two-one-two arrangement of design elements, the "two's" being the white squares on the top and bottom and the "one" the motif in the center. (This kind of design is related to a Turkish rug design called a large-patterned Holbein, and possibly indicates some Turkish influence.) The white octagon in the center rests upon a checkerboard pattern, which focuses attention on it. Inside the white octagon is a red octagon, and inside this, concentrically, is a gold octagon that encloses a diamond, which marks the center of the design with a cross. Surrounding this hypnotic activity, rectangles, hooked motifs, stars, animals, and other motifs fill all the rest of the available space in the field in a beautifully balanced way. Nothing in this design hovers discreetly in the background. Each part comes forth directly. Yet there is great subtlety, too. Notice, for instance, how in the center motif the red octagon and four red squares echo in miniature the larger white octagon and squares of the field. The border is a simple setting for the active design. The colors are complementary to those of the field.

Though the needlepoint necessarily does not have the pile or large scale of the original knotted Kazak, the design works well in this version. Using #8 penelope canvas would come closer to the size of the original rug, but it would require piecing. The size given is an adaptation of the design for a single width of mono canvas.

Color

Color	Principal Colors (11)		Auxiliary Colors (9)	
	Amount	Paternayan Yarn No.	Amount	Paternayan Yarn No.
dark brown	1 lb.	**112**	1 oz.	113
ivory	¾ lb.	**492**		
red	1 lb.	**267**	¼ lb.	210
			1½ oz.	207
gold	2 oz.	**462**	1 oz.	466
green	10 oz.	**340**	2 oz.	367
			1 oz.	516
dark blue	¼ lb.	**365**	1 oz.	311
medium blue	2 oz.	**334**	1 oz.	314
dark gold	1 oz.	**145**		
light green	2 oz.	**512**	2 oz.	560
maroon	2 oz.	**201**		
violet	1 oz.	**123**		

A variety of greens were used in the background of the field. 340 was mixed in varying amounts with 367 and 516. A horizontal band of light green abrash worked in 560 was included to re-create the feeling of the original. For less contrast, mix 560 with 512.

In the field 267 was mixed with 210. To darken the red in the main border it was mixed with 207.

Use the darker shades of blue, 365 and 311, in the field; mix them with the lighter shades, 334 and 314, in the border.

The same general observation holds true for this rug as for other rugs in this book: you can create an equally excellent piece without mixing colors.

Directions

1. Prepare a piece of #10 mono canvas 54″ by 66″ (137.2 cm by 167.6 cm).

2. Mark the corresponding (heavy) graph lines.

3. Mark the center horizontal and vertical threads of the canvas.

4. Mark the outer edge of the design. The graph thread count is 473 by 617. There are 236 horizontal stitches on either side of the center thread and 308 vertical stitches on either side of the center thread.

5. Mark the dividing lines of the border. Start from the outer edge, using the following table:

Outer edge	**1 stitch**
Band of squares	2 stitches
Dividing line	**1 stitch**
Counterchange band	11 stitches
Dividing line	**1 stitch**
Band of squares	2 stitches
Dividing line	**1 stitch**
Wine cup border	40 stitches
Dividing line	**1 stitch**
Band of squares	2 stitches
Dividing line	**1 stitch**
Counterchange band	11 stitches
Dividing line	**1 stitch**
Band of squares	2 stitches
Dividing line (field line)	**1 stitch**
Total width of border =	78 stitches

6. Put in the center diamond. Mark the large rectangle, the octagons, and the diamond and hooked motifs.

7. Place the large squares in each corner, and mark one or two stars. The remainder can be stitched directly.

8. Mark the remaining small rectangular motifs in the field. *Note:* The gold "vase-shaped" motif is designed with an even number of stitches and will contain one more stitch to the left of the center.

9. Work the central medallion, using Color Plate C–8 as a guide. To stitch the checkers, work the small squares in diagonal rows with red and blue yarn.

10. Work the remainder of the field, outlining first and filling in later. Where there is no outline for the animals, stitch the entire shape before you fill in the background.

11. Note that two different animals appear in the field. To more easily place them, indicate the rectangles into which they fit. Those in the horizontal rows of four are larger and have different horns than the others. Draw this rectangle lightly *between* the threads of the canvas and then stitch the animal directly on the canvas.

12. Work the main and guard borders, following the graph. Note the slight adjustments in the spacing between the motifs on the side borders and within the motifs on the top and bottom borders.

13. Work the rug, following the graph for the lower half of the design.

14. After you have completed this portion, you may turn the graph upside down and work the upper portion. The motifs will be exactly the same, but their position on the graph will be different. The animals will always stand with their feet down, and the horizontal band of abrash does not appear.

15. Stitch one extra row of red around the outer edge of the finished rug. Work the binding stitches into that row.

Design Ideas for Coordinate Patterns

Use the central medallion as an individual design.

Use the corner medallions individually or together in a repeating design.

Make an all-over pattern of the animals for a small piece.

An interesting pattern would be formed if the counterchange guard bands were placed adjacently.

Construct an all-over pattern of large diamonds using the motifs of the main border in adjacent rows.

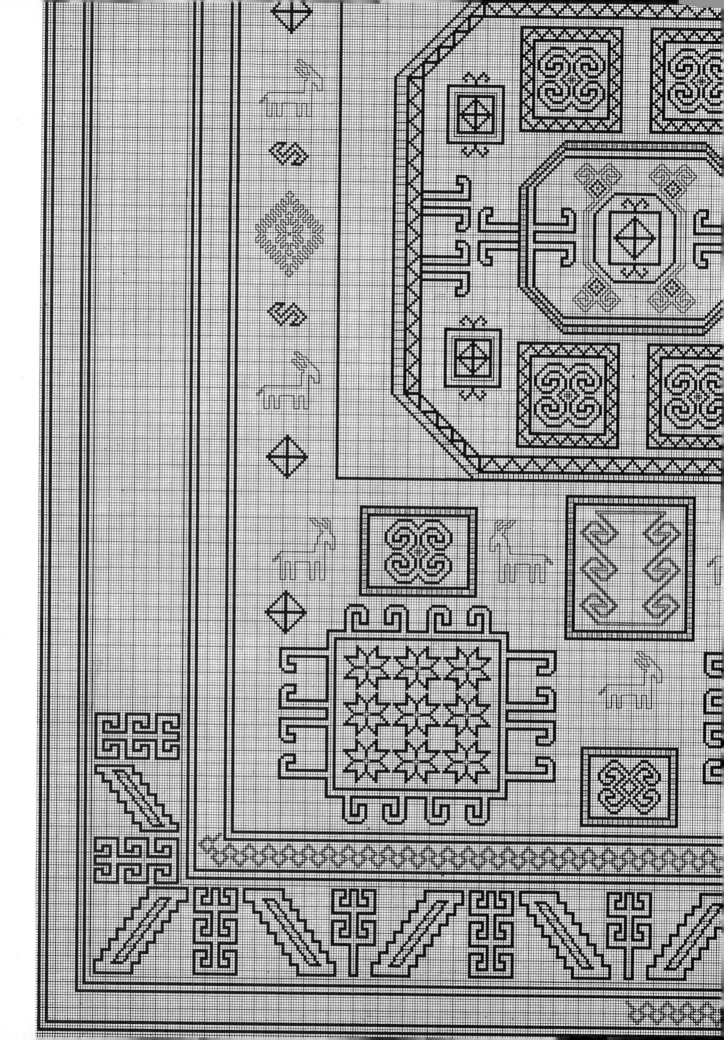

C-1. Shirvan Rug. See pages 23–32. Stitched by Norma Braverman.

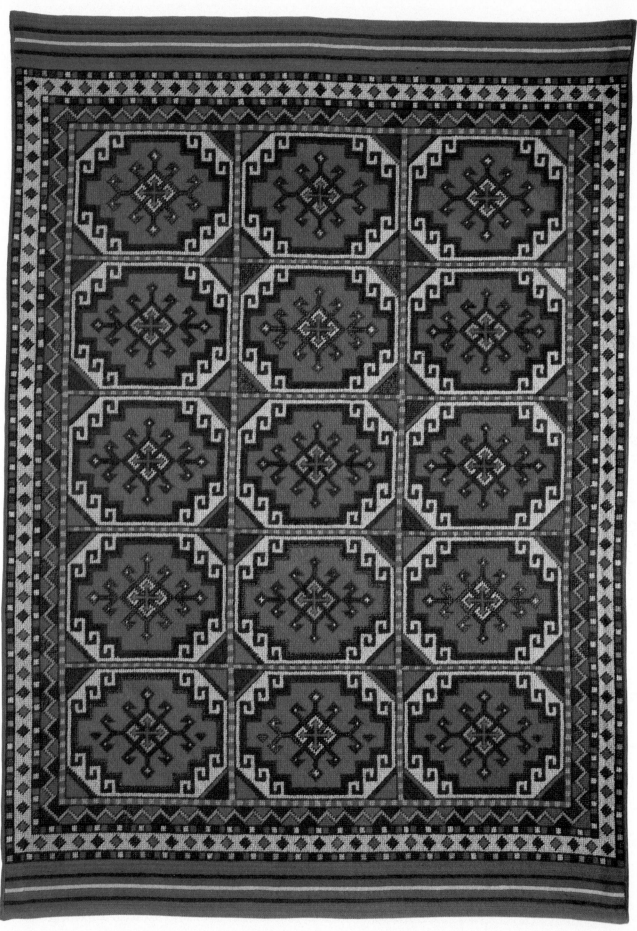

C–2. Caucasian Rug. See pages 33–39. Stitched by Lillian Schoenfeld.

C-3. Lotto Rug. See pages 90–101. Stitched by Elinor and Nancy Migdal.

C–4. Transylvanian Rug. See pages 77–89. Stitched by Mae Eisenberg.

C-5. Rug with Spots and Stripes. See pages 58–66. Stitched by Marie Love.

C–6. Turkish Prayer Rug. See pages 67–76. Stitched by Shirley Wiesen.

C–7. Lesghi Star Rug. See pages 49–57. Stitched by Selwyn Cooper.

C–8. Geometrical Kazak Rug. See pages 40–48. Stitched by Jerry Levine.

LESGHI STAR RUG

44″ by 73″ (102 cm × 185 cm) on #8 penelope canvas

The heavens figure predominantly in Islam—as reflected by its discoveries in the field of astronomy and, symbolically, in its art, an example of which is the unusual star motif in this rug. Though somewhat rare in a Kazak rug, the star motif was popular throughout the Caucasus.

The Lesghi star is the large, steplike star motif that has twelve points on its outer perimeter. (*Lesghi* is the name of a mountain tribe; it also came to be used as a general term for "mountaineer.") Three Lesghi stars appear in the field, enclosing large blue stars, which in turn enclose smaller stars. The colors of these large central stars interact closely with the background, especially the center star, which is a subtle green-blue. Dark blue is an unusual background color in an Oriental rug. Here it provides an appropriate nocturnal setting.

Many motifs surround these stars in a partially symmetrical, partially random arrangement. Of these motifs, the "house," which contains the date of stitching (in Arabic in the original), is probably intended to be a church, indicating this particular rug was woven by Christians. Note the square in the very center of the rug. It contains all the colors of the design and may have served as a color card or sampler for the weaver.

The eight-pointed star of the motif is repeated in smaller size in the border. I find particularly resonant the use of the light blue of two of the large stars for the ground in the border. The star border is one that is often used in Caucasian weaving. Here, each of the randomly colored stars contains a diamond and has a single sparkling stitch of white at each point. When stitching parts like this, I like to outline many of them first. Then I fill several needles with different colors, and enjoy intuitively selecting one fill-in color after another.

Color

	Principal Colors (6)		Auxiliary Colors (6)	
Color	Amount	Paternayan Yarn No.	Amount	Paternayan Yarn No.
dark brown	1 lb.	112		
blue	1¼ lbs.	311	¼ lb.	365
			¼ lb.	305
light blue	¾ lb.	314	¼ lb.	380
ivory	6 oz.	492		
red	¾ lb.	267	2 oz.	210
			2 oz.	207
green	2 oz.	340	1 oz.	512

Particularly effective is the subtle interplay created between the central blue-green star and the blue background. Work the central star with a mixture of 311 (blue) and 340 (green). Work the background with 311 and 365, and small amounts of 305. The dark blue, 305, is used more often in the border.

The darker shade of red, 207, does not appear in the field but is used in the border.

A variety of colors and shades are used in the small triangles in the guard band. You can be quite free here; use bits and pieces of leftover yarn.

Directions

1. Prepare a piece of #8 penelope canvas 50″ by 79″ (127 cm by 201 cm).

2. Mark the corresponding (heavy) graph lines.

3. Mark the center horizontal and vertical threads of the canvas.

4. Mark the outer edge of the design. The graph thread count is 351 by 583. Horizontally, there are 175 stitches on either side of the center thread. Vertically, there are 291 stitches on either side of the center thread.

5. Mark the dividing lines of the border. Start from the outer edge, using the following table.

Outer edge	**2 stitches**
Band of squares	2 stitches
Dividing line	**2 stitches**
Triangular band	6 stitches
Dividing line	**1 stitch**
Star border	23 stitches
Dividing line	**1 stitch**
Band of squares	2 stitches
Dividing line	**1 stitch**
Triangular band	6 stitches
Dividing line	**1 stitch**
Red stripe	1 stitch
Dividing line (field line)	**1 stitch**

Total width of border = 49 stitches

6. Outline the center checkered square, the star, and the enclosing square.

7. Continue marking the three large medallions (Lesghi stars). Mark the center one first, then each of the other two.

8. When you have finished outlining this portion of your design, fill in the shapes with colored yarn, using Color Plate C–7 as a guide.

9. Put in the surrounding diamond motifs. Fill in the background, working outward from field to side borders.

10. Outline the remaining field motifs. Fill in the Lesghi stars, field motifs, and background in the same manner, from the center out toward the borders.

11. Outline the guard bands and the main border. Fill in using the sample rug, or your intuition, as a guide.

12. Stitch an extra row of red around the perimeter of the finished rug. Bind with the same color yarn.

Design Ideas for Coordinate Patterns

Use a single Lesghi Star medallion for an individual piece.

Make an all-over pattern of the border stars.

Repeat and vary the square panel within the Lesghi Star, creating a patchwork-like pattern.

Place the motifs from the field randomly on a blue background.

Turkish Rugs

If Caucasian rugs such as these first four were little known in the West until relatively recent times, the opposite is true of Turkish rugs, such as the next six. Anatolia, the land now called Turkey, was once the heart of the Byzantine Empire and has been a bridge between East and West for thousands of years. A large body of geometric patterns found their way into Turkish weaving traditions, and the earliest Oriental rugs known in Europe came from there. A special familiarity with Turkish rugs continued from the thirteenth century onward. Those are the rugs which most frequently appear in European painting. Sometimes European noblemen even ordered custom-made Turkish carpets with their coat of arms woven in. Turkey was also the conduit for European rug trading with the rest of the Near East.

Also in contrast to Caucasian rugs, which were relatively free of outside influences, are the many influences apparent in the rugs of Turkey. As conquests occurred, each regime had an impact upon rug design. Rugs woven for the courts of the rulers influenced even rural and village rugs. The early Turkish rugs were simple geometric designs, and as one follows their history, their influence, too, becomes clear. New levels of sophistication were incorporated into the bold designs and brilliant colors of Turkish rugs, but they retained their basic energy. No wonder that by the sixteenth century they became so expensive that only the wealthiest Europeans could afford them.

■ dark brown
□ ivory
• red

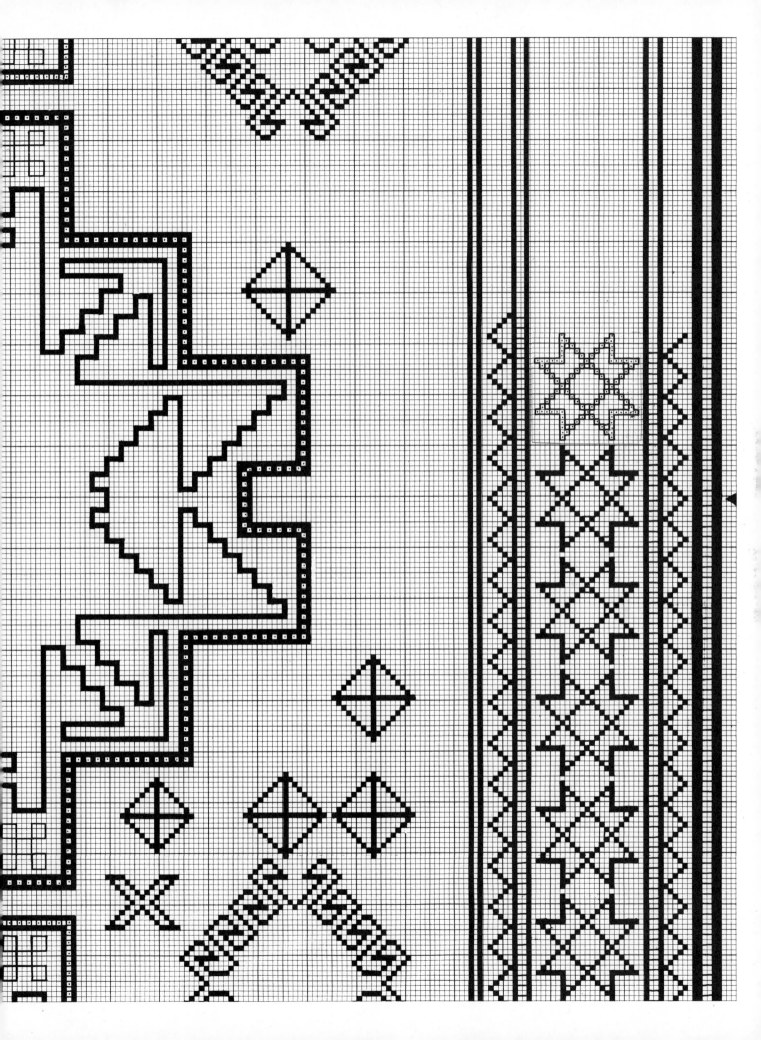

RUG WITH SPOTS AND STRIPES

47″ by 70″ (119 cm × 178 cm) on #10 mono canvas

The spot-and-stripe motif of this Turkish rug appears more frequently than any other in the court art—ceramics, carpets, silks, and other textiles—of the Ottoman Empire. The exact origin of this simple design is obscure, but one theory is that it is derived from animal skins—tiger stripes and leopard spots. These skins were symbols of prestige and authority in the Near East and Central Asia. The pelts were sometimes used as rugs.

Carpets of this type are known to have been woven in the late sixteenth and early seventeenth centuries and are very valuable. Scholars find these rugs particularly fascinating but potentially hazardous to identify; a curator of the Victoria and Albert Museum in London lost his job for purchasing a forgery of this design. A forgery in this case means a rug that was woven later, usually in the late nineteenth or early twentieth century, but is passed off as an authentic early rug. One giveaway is that a later rug contains chemical dyes, which were not invented until the middle of the nineteenth century. Another clue is the suspiciously good condition of many forgeries, although holes, repairs, and other damages are sometimes cleverly faked. Because of the rarity of the originals, and the demand for them, forgeries are probably at least as common as the genuine article.

In the original design of this rug the wavy line and triangular ball arrangement in the field is usually limited to three colors: predominantly red and green, with some yellow. In planning the coloring of this adaptation it occurred to me that a random use of a greater number of colors in the stripes might work well. I decided, perhaps irreverently, to try it, but I think the greater variety adds interest to the stitching of this large repeating design. In this version, the balls are filled in with dark brown. In the original version, each ball had an eye in its center (see Figure 3–3). This is an option you may wish to use, perhaps with a color variation.

The restraint and simplicity of the field are complemented by an extraordinary border. It is anything but restrained or simple, but it successfully completes the design. It is made up of "cloud bands" (the larger motif) and blossoming vines, which are randomly and very colorfully filled in. A small vine appears in the guard bands. I think you will enjoy the unfolding of the color changes as you stitch this border. The ivory ground acts as a bastion of stability, holding the design together. The use of ivory for the ground is unusual among Oriental rugs, doubly so because the same ground color is used in both border and field.

Color

| Color | Principal Colors (12) | | Auxiliary Colors (2) | |
	Amount	Paternayan Yarn No.	Amount	Paternayan Yarn No.
dark brown	1 lb.	112	1 lb.	113
ivory	3 lbs.	136		
red	2 oz.	267		
dark red	2 oz.	207		
blue	1 oz.	311		
light blue	1 oz.	314		
gold	3 oz.	433		
dark gold	¼ lb.	145		
green	2 oz.	512	12 strands	560
olive	1 oz.	540		
light brown	1 oz.	104		
salmon	1 oz.	274		

The lighter brown, 113, is actually the original's brown-black, which has faded. For stronger contrast, omit 113 and use 112 throughout the rug. No other particular color suggestions are necessary for this rug. Use the colors given. The combinations create a wonderful harmony. The guard bands present a good opportunity to use bits and pieces of left-over yarn.

The differences in the shades of ivory in the background that can be seen in the color plate are variations in the dye lots of the yarn, and not a new color. They approximate the natural shadings of undyed wool.

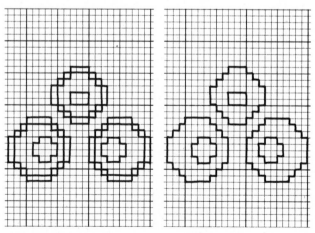

3–3. Triple ball motif with "eyes" drawn with and without an outline.

58

Directions

1. Prepare a piece of #10 mono canvas 54″ by 76″ (137 cm by 193 cm).

2. Mark the corresponding (heavy) graph lines.

3. Mark the center horizontal and vertical threads of the canvas.

4. Mark the outer edge of the design. The graph thread count is 469 by 699. Horizontally, there are 234 stitches on either side of the center thread. Vertically, there are 349 stitches on either side of the center thread.

5. Mark the dividing lines of the border. Start from the outer edge, using the following table.

Outer edge	**1 stitch**
Leaf border	11 stitches
Dividing line	**1 stitch**
Cloud band border	56 stitches
Dividing line	**1 stitch**
Leaf border	11 stitches
Dividing line (field line)	**1 stitch**
Total width of border =	82 stitches

6. Put in the three balls at the center, and continue marking the motifs vertically downward along the central axis. Rows 1, 3, and 5 are in the same position as each other on the graph. Rows 2 and 4 are what is known as a half-drop repeat and are in the same position as each other.

7. Outline the remaining motifs on the bottom of the graph. When you have finished, continue working upward until you reach the top of the field, using the graph as a guide.

8. If you are stitching directly, I recommend that you begin filling the motifs and the background before you outline the entire design. This will prevent unnecessary handling of the already stitched portion. Use Color Plate C-5, and your intuition, as a guide.

9. Outline the main border. When you have completed the bottom half, turn the graph upside down and work the upper half. The motifs will be exactly the same, but their position on the graph will be different. Follow the motifs, but disregard their position on the graph underneath. Make sure the center of the graph corresponds to the center (horizontal and vertical) threads of the canvas.

10. With needles threaded with different colored yarns, fill in the motifs in the border.

11. Work the guard bands. Their random coloring makes them fun to stitch, and almost any color combination will look good. They are designed continuously, not symmetrically. All eight corners are different. The upper corners do not appear on the graph. They are given in figures 3-4, 3-5, 3-6, and 3-7.

12. Stitch two extra rows of ivory around the outer edge of the finished rug. Bind directly into the last row.

Design Ideas for Coordinate Patterns

Use the motifs of the field for an all-over pattern.

Use the border pattern for a long narrow design (a bolster or upholstery for a director's chair).

Invert every other row of the leaf guard band to create a striped pattern.

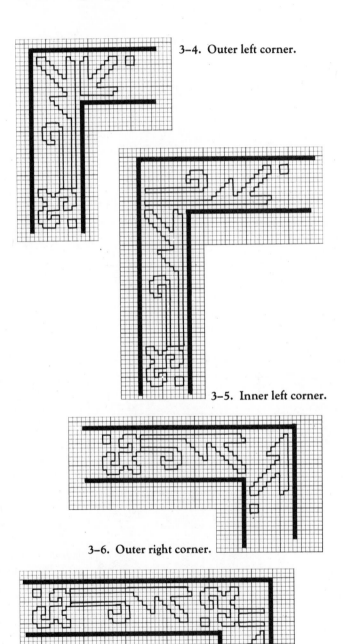

3-4. Outer left corner.

3-5. Inner left corner.

3-6. Outer right corner.

3-7. Inner right corner.

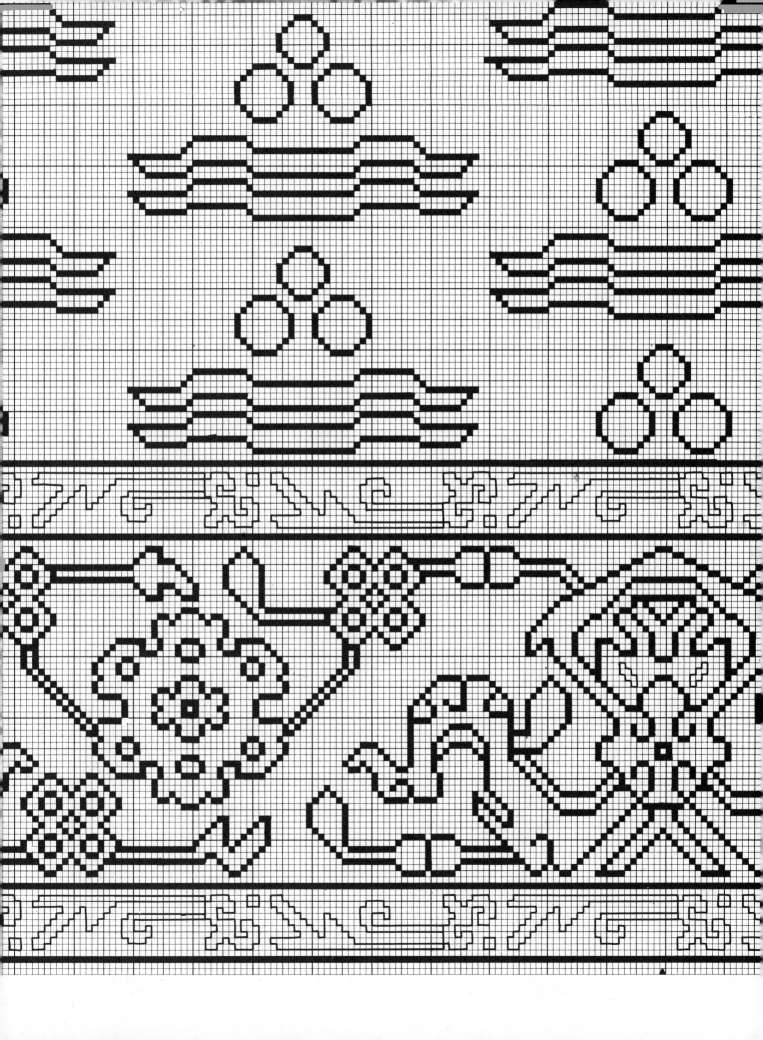

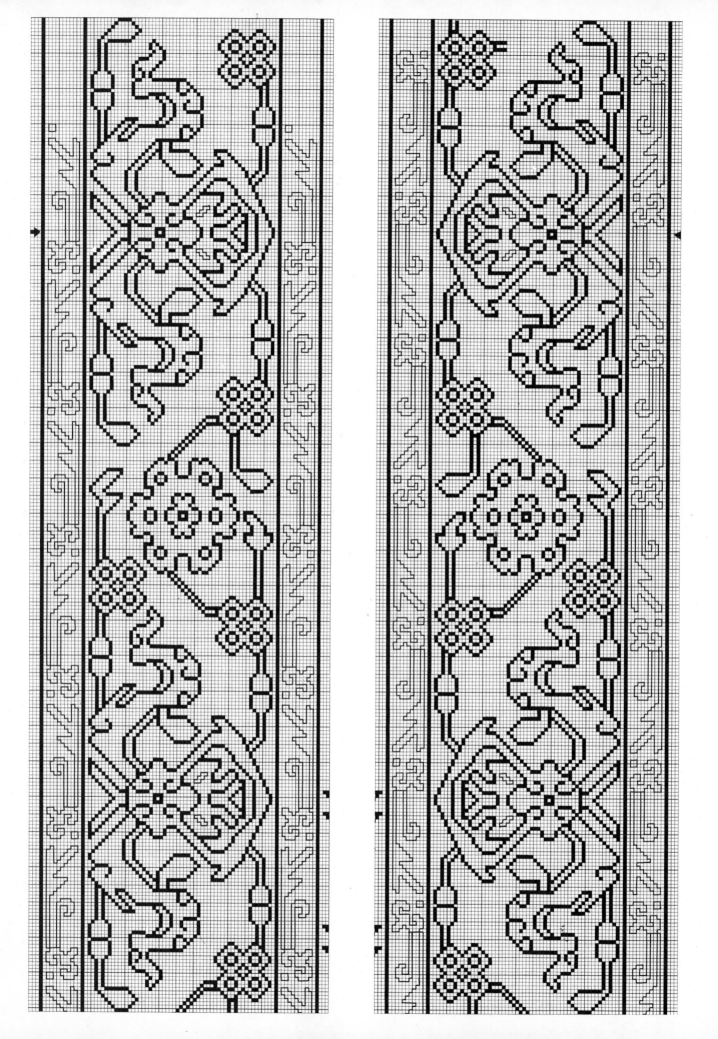

TURKISH PRAYER RUG

44" by 63" (112 cm × 160 cm) on #8 penelope canvas

In Islam, a requisite for prayer is that one find a "clean piece of ground" on which to kneel. A small rug placed anywhere on the ground fills this need. Theoretically any rug will do, but in practice, a prayer rug is of a particular design: two columns on either side of the field supporting an arch at the top. In mosques there is a wall niche, called the Mihrab, with an arch that indicates the direction of Mecca. It is generally thought that the design of prayer rugs represents this niche, though in its translation to this medium the design has undergone many transformations, as this rug and the next one demonstrate. Though very different, both are derived from the basic prayer rug form. The arch is construed by some to represent the doorway to Paradise, which can be entered through prayer. If the field is filled with flowers (as it is in this and the next rug), it may be considered representation of Paradise itself, which is described in the Koran as a garden filled with flowering plants and softly flowing brooks.

In this version of the prayer rug, the arch is eliminated and the columns are made the focus of the design. At each side, and in the center of the field, are elongated shrubs that grow out of vases at the bottom. The triple suspended shapes between the columns are thought to represent mosque lamps, very much abstracted. In the original there was a flat panel supported by the columns at the top of the field, which enclosed a repeating motif. I eliminated it in my graph for purposes of symmetry, but I have graphed it separately for those who would like to include it, or who simply wish to be informed about the original design (see figure 3–8). If you do wish to include it, the interspacing of the elements in the field will have to be adjusted (see Directions, step 15).

The floral subtheme of the field is brought to the forefront in the border in the repeated large rosettes of the main border and the smaller rosettes of the guard bands. The guard bands were a mystery to me during my research. When I charted this rug I looked at the original and saw what I assumed to be a repeating pattern of rosettes with intermittent spaces between groups of the motif. This is the way the rug appeared to have been stitched. But the arrangement seemed out of character. When making the final graph I inspected a color print of the original with a magnifying glass. I found that what looked like spaces to the naked eye were actually faded yellow rosettes on a yellow ground. Of these, only the centers remained clearly visible. In the graph I have included all the rosettes, which accounts for the discrepancy between it and the stitched rug in Color Plate 6. The regular color sequence of every other rosette being a red one is used in a variation in the main border and the guard bands. This sequence is indicated on the graph.

Color

Color	Principal Colors (7)		Auxiliary Colors (5)	
	Amount	Paternayan Yarn No.	Amount	Paternayan Yarn No.
brown-black	¾ lb.	105		
yellow	2½ lbs.	445	½ oz.	433
red	½ lb.	267	2 oz.	207
blue	¼ lb.	311	1 oz.	314
			1 oz.	380
salmon	2 oz.	245		
dark gold	¾ lb.	521	¼ lb.	145
ivory	¼ lb.	136		

Work the rosettes, which are omitted in the guard band in the sample rug (but are included in the graph), in 433. Work the background in 445. The rosettes will be very subtle, but there nevertheless, a pale, shadowy presence.

Red 267 is darkened with 207.

Blue 311 is lightened with 314 and 380.

Avoid using mixed strands of yarn for outlining.

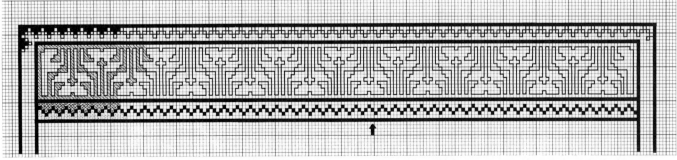

3–8. **This panel may be placed at the top of the field. Put it directly below the innermost zigzag band of the border, as shown.**

Directions

1. Prepare a piece of #8 penelope canvas 51″ by 69″ (130 cm by 175 cm).

2. Mark the corresponding (heavy) graph lines.

3. Mark the center horizontal and vertical threads of the canvas.

4. Mark the outer edge of the design. The graph thread count is 349 by 501. Horizontally, there are 174 stitches on either side of the center thread. Vertically, there are 250 stitches on either side of the center thread.

5. Mark the dividing lines of the border. Start from the outer edge, using the following table.

Outer edge	**1 stitch**
Zigzag strip	4 stitches
Dividing line	**1 stitch**
Rosette band	11 stitches
Dividing line	**1 stitch**
Zigzag strip	4 stitches
Dividing line	**1 stitch**
Large rosette border	37 stitches
Dividing line	**1 stitch**
Zigzag strip	4 stitches
Dividing line	**1 stitch**
Rosette band	11 stitches
Dividing line	**1 stitch**
Zigzag strip	4 stitches
Dividing line (field line)	**1 stitch**
Total width of border =	83 stitches

6. Put in the central vase and flowering shrubs that run along the central axis.

7. Outline the four symmetrical columns, the "mosque lamps," and the remaining vases and shrubs.

8. Turn the graph upside down to complete the details of the four columns.

9. When this outlining is completed, fill in the motifs and the background with colored yarn, using Color Plate C–6 as a guide.

10. With ivory 136 work the zigzag outline in the guard bands. Fill in one side with brown-black 105 and the other with red 267.

11. Outline the red, blue, and salmon rosettes in the main border with brown-black. Stitch the outline of the dark gold rosettes with red yarn.

12. To work the rest of the main border, turn the graph upside down. Use the colors in the sample rug as a guide.

13. Fill in the flowers, leaves, and background.

14. Work the narrow border rosettes, following the graph rather than the color plate. Turn the graph upside down to work the upper portion of the border, continuing the color sequence as given.

15. If you choose to include the panel (see figure 3–8), shorten the columns at the center, reduce the number of stitches between the "mosque lamps" by five, and omit one pair of blossoms on the vertical shrubs. Fill in the panel, following the color code.

16. Stitch one extra row of ivory 136 around the outer edge of the finished rug. Bind into that row with gold 445.

Design Ideas for Coordinate Patterns

Create an all-over pattern using the large rosettes of the border. The following color sequence would make a nice design.

row 1: red yellow pink blue
row 2: pink blue red yellow

Repeat the pattern, in alternating rows.

Make a design using the smaller rosettes of the guard bands. If you omit the zigzag strips it will be an all-over pattern; if you include them, it will be a striped pattern.

Design a striped pattern with the blossoming vines of the field.

■	brown-black
□	ivory
⊡	red
⊠	blue
◩	dark gold

TRANSYLVANIAN RUG
48″ by 66″ (122 cm × 168 cm) on #10 mono canvas

Most prayer rugs have one arch at the top of the field, with columns to support it. In this prayer rug, the dark corners of the field form *two* arches, one right side up and the other upside down. This kind of mirror-image symmetry is a common device of Oriental rug design. The drawing of every element in the upper half of the field in this rug is mirrored by the lower half, though the coloring varies.

The fact that this is indeed a prayer rug is somewhat concealed. The columns, present in many prayer rugs, are omitted here. Though the appearance of the yellow area of the field seems to resemble a medallion design (like that of the Turkish Mat, in which the central design is a single motif), in reality its derivation is quite different.

Hanging in the center of each arch is a vase-shaped lamp from which issues a bouquet of fabulous flowers. The device of the lamp, which is often used, is thought to have been inspired by a passage from the Koran: *Allah is the light of the heavens and the earth; a likeness of his light is as a niche in which there is a lamp.*

This wonderfully complex design has layer upon layer of detail. Notice, for instance, how the ivory-colored cartouche panels of the border echo the large yellow shape of the field. Or how richly and successfully the arabesques of the corner spandrels enclose the design of the field. These arabesques, which derive from leaf forms, reinforce the floral motifs of the field and then are restated in the arabesques of the border, from which blossoms sprout. In the guard bands are "reciprocal trefoils," that is, the black shapes are trefoils, and the red shapes are also trefoils, and they fit together in a jigsaw-puzzle-like way.

The Transylvanian Rug is named for a region of Rumania where many such rugs were found in churches. It is thought that they were donated in memory of deceased parishioners. The original from which this rug was adapted is believed to have been made in the seventeenth century, when this region was part of the Ottoman Empire. Either the rugs were brought from Turkey, or the cottage industry of rugmaking itself was transplanted for a time.

Color

Color	Amount	Paternayan Yarn No.	Amount	Paternayan Yarn No.
gold	1½ lbs.	**433**		
red	¾ lb.	**267**	¾ lb.	210
blue	½ lb.	**311**	1 oz.	365
yellow	2 oz.	**445**		
dark green	1 oz.	**512**		
light green	1 oz.	**516**		
dark gold	2 oz.	**145**		

For an even quality, omit the shading in the background. Use 433 by itself. Use 145 mixed with 433 where a darker gold is needed to fill in a motif.

Color variations enliven the repeating pattern of the border. Use bits and pieces of leftover yarn. Also, note the changes in color in the outlines.

Directions

1. Prepare a piece of #10 mono canvas 54″ by 72″ (137 cm by 183 cm).

2. Mark the corresponding (heavy) graph lines.

3. Mark the center horizontal and vertical threads of the canvas.

4. Mark the outer edge of the design. The graph thread count is 479 by 655. Horizontally, there are 239 stitches on either side of the center thread. Vertically, there are 327 stitches on either side of the center thread.

5. Mark the dividing lines of the border. Start from the outer edge, using the following table.

Outer edge (brown-black)	**1 stitch**
Dividing line (ivory)	**1 stitch**
Narrow chain band	7 stitches
Dividing line (brown-black)	**1 stitch**
Dividing line (ivory)	1 stitch
Reciprocal trefoil	20 stitches
Dividing line (ivory)	**1 stitch**
Dividing line (brown-black)	**1 stitch**
Cartouche and star border	61 stitches
Dividing line (brown-black)	**1 stitch**
Dividing line (ivory)	1 stitch
Reciprocal trefoil	20 stitches
Dividing line (ivory)	**1 stitch**

(Table continued on next page)

Color

	Principal Colors (9)		Auxiliary Colors (3)	
Color	Amount	Paternayan Yarn No.	Amount	Paternayan Yarn No.
brown-black	1 lb.	**105**	6 oz.	112
ivory	1½ lbs.	**136**		

77

Dividing line (brown-black)	**1 stitch**
Dividing line (red)	**1 stitch**
Narrow chain band	7 stitches
Dividing line (red)	**1 stitch**
Dividing line (brown-black)	**1 stitch**
Dividing line (ivory)	**1 stitch**
Dividing line (brown-black; field line)	**1 stitch**
Total width of border =	130 stitches

6. Outline the arches at either end of the design. A single row of brown-black, two rows of ivory, one row of brown-black, followed by a row of red, separates these corner spandrels from the remainder of the field.

7. Work the central portion of the field. Outline the vase-shaped lamps, the flowers, and the leaves. Change the colors of the outlines as indicated on the graph, but keep the drawing of the pattern count the same.

8. With ivory, outline the arabesques in the four corner spandrels. Turn the canvas upside down to work the upper ones. Disregard the positioning on the graph, which will be correct in the lower portion only.

9. When the outlining is complete, fill in the motifs and the background with colored yarn, using Color Plate C–4 as a guide.

10. Outline the adjacent narrow chain border with ivory. (If you choose to simplify the design, omit the small white dots in the center of the chain.)

11. Work the trefoil border.

12. Outline the main border. First mark, then stitch, the heavy brown-black line forming the stars and cartouches. Stitch the appropriate ivory and red rows on either side.

13. In the border, work the medallions within the stars and the arabesques within the cartouches. Vary the outlines and colors as indicated on the lower portion of the graph. These can add individuality to your rug.

14. Work the checkered leaf motif between the stars and cartouches. Fill in the background with gold 433.

15. Complete the border and stitch one row of red and two rows of dark gold around the perimeter of the design. Bind the rug in dark gold.

16. Stitch one extra row of red and two extra rows of gold around the outer edge of the finished rug. Bind with gold yarn.

Design Ideas for Coordinate Patterns

Use the mosque lamp and flowers of the field for an individual piece. You may embellish with additional flowers in the same style.

Make a runner or mat using the border pattern on a larger gauge canvas.

Design a smaller piece using a single motif from the border (small pillow, pin cushion, or coaster).

Create an all-over counterchange pattern by mirroring and repeating the reciprocal trefoils of the guard bands.

Make a small geometric pattern using the narrow chain bands.

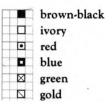

brown-black
ivory
red
blue
green
gold

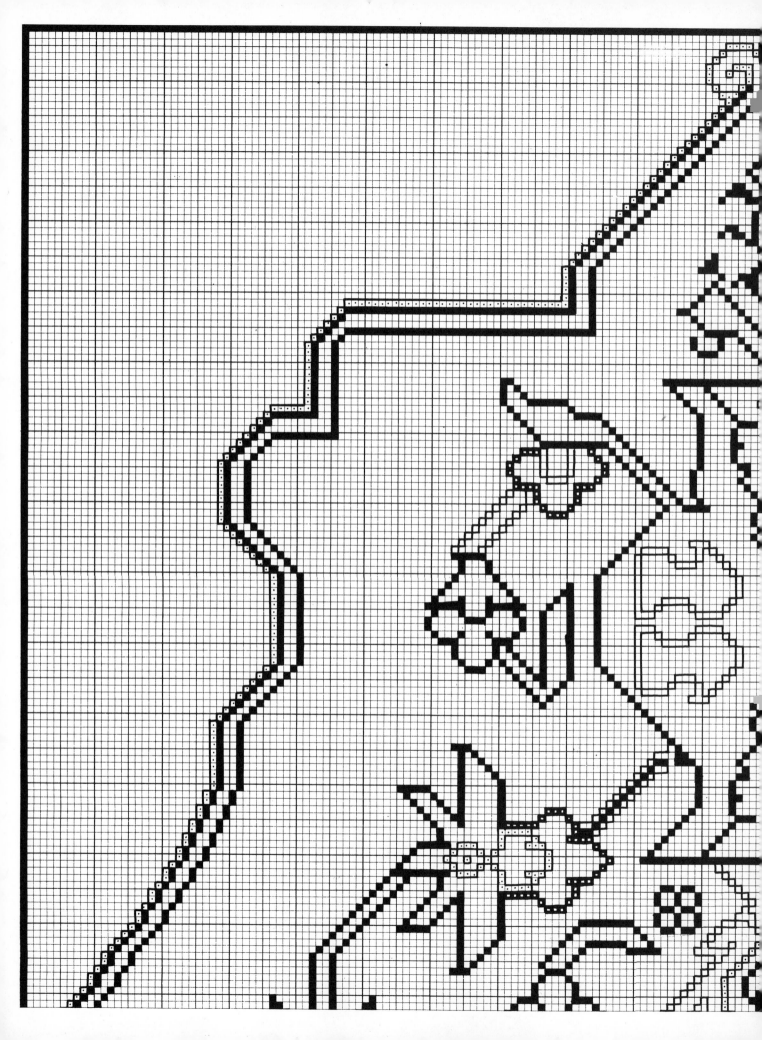

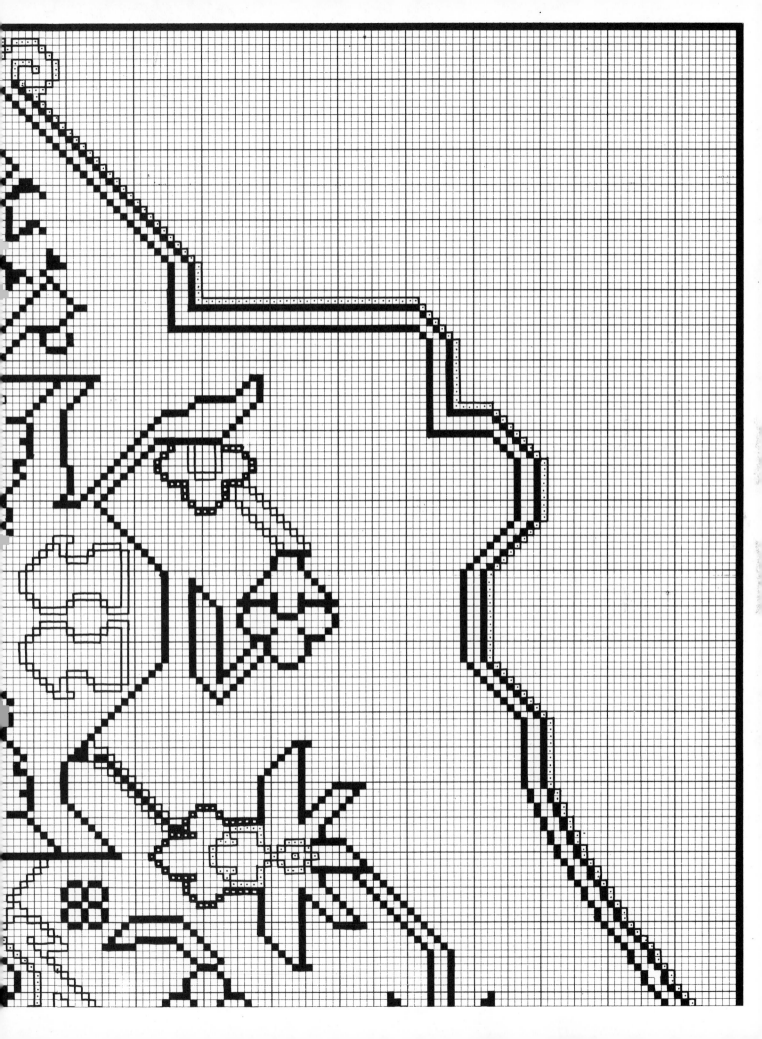

LOTTO RUG

43″ by 61″ (109 cm × 155 cm) on #8 penelope canvas or #10 mono canvas

(This design looks well on either canvas; the penelope is closer in scale to the original, but the mono will be easier to see when marking the outline.)

The spectacular red and gold latticelike pattern that has come to be called *Lotto* is, for me, one of the most fascinating carpet designs. I have looked at many Oriental rugs with an eye to graphing them, so I am accustomed to identifying the underlying structure, and once I find it, my task of charting is much easier. But this pattern is so carefully balanced and the elements so artfully juxtaposed that I have never been able to say that I have found the single key to its construction to my complete satisfaction. I have looked at this and other Lotto carpets for many hours with growing interest, often discovering new things. Sometimes, when I squint, I see whole series of hidden relationships. Because of the many ways it can be seen, it is a difficult pattern to describe. The repeat, for instance, is concealed from easy view. Actually, one needs to know only a relatively small portion of the apparently complicated pattern in order to make the whole design. This segment is then mirrored and repeated (see figure 3–9).

The name of these rugs is derived from that of Lorenzo Lotto, the fifteenth-century Italian artist who depicted them in his paintings. They have had other more descriptive names, but this convenient one has become common. Designs of the Lotto type have appeared in many versions, with more or less of the repeat used. Usually this variation is not achieved by enlarging or reducing the size of the motif but by making the field larger or smaller. The larger the field, the more repeats will be included. It is often amazing to see how this can transform the pattern. Especially in small versions where less of the repeat is visible, the same Lotto motif can seem to create a totally different design.

The details of a Lotto carpet also vary from one to another. In this one, many of the diagonal lines have a sawtooth appearance. This may identify it as having been made in Transylvania when that region was under Turkish influence. Another detail, which I omitted from the graph for purposes of clarity, are little white squares, attached to the gold lattice. They are shown in figure 3–9. If you wish to make your rug more authentic, you may include them by repeating the positioning shown throughout the field.

The elegant border of this rug echoes the latticelike feeling of the field with ivory-colored arabesques. The dark ground makes a clear frame for the Lotto design. Some elements of the border are worked with an

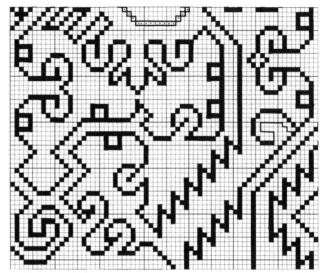

3–9. Repeating elements of the Lotto pattern, showing the placement of the small white squares.

outline and some without, as indicated on the graph. This dazzling border pattern could be very nicely worked as an all-over design in its own right (see figure 3–10).

Because of the many twistings and turnings of this rug design, outlining it requires particular attention. A greater amount of maneuvering, looking, and counting is called for. You may find that coloring the design with waterproof markers, or even painting it on the canvas, are helpful measures. Once the outline is done, filling in a Lotto pattern is pure pleasure. It is a delight to see the design come forward and recede, emerge and develop, continuing to reveal new aspects of its complexity.

Color

| Color | Principal Colors (8) | | Auxiliary Colors (4) | |
	Amount	Paternayan Yarn No.	Amount	Paternayan Yarn No.
dark brown	½ lb.	114		
red	1 lb.	210	3 oz.	267
gold	¾ lb.	462	1 oz.	433
medium blue	3 oz.	311	25 strands	365
light blue	2 oz.	314	2 oz.	380
dark blue	½ lb.	305		
ivory	¼ lb.	136		
green	2 oz.	516	1 oz.	512

3–10. The arabesque border as an all-over pattern. Additional "s"-like forms were added for further interest.

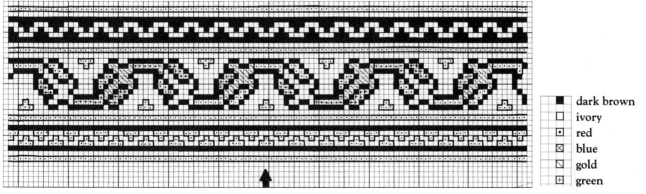

	dark brown
	ivory
	red
	blue
	gold
	green

3–11. This band would be placed both inside and outside the main arabesque border. The upper zigzag band coincides with the zigzag band on the graph. Change the coloring, as indicated on this figure.

For a lighter color feeling in the field, use 466 instead of 462 and omit the auxiliary color 433.

Use 311 and 365 for the dark blue motifs in the field. Use 305 with small amounts of 311 and 365 in the background of the border. Use 314 in the field. Mix it with 380 in the border.

Directions

1. Prepare a piece of either #10 mono canvas 40″ by 55″ (102 cm by 140 cm) or #8 penelope canvas 49″ by 67″ (125 cm by 170 cm).

2. Mark the corresponding (heavy) graph lines.

3. Mark the center horizontal and vertical threads of the canvas.

4. Mark the outer edge of the design. The graph thread count is 343 by 487. Horizontally, there are 171 stitches on either side of the center thread. Vertically, there are 243 stitches on either side of the center thread.

5. Mark the dividing lines of the border. Start from the outer edge, using the following table.

Outer edge (red)	1 stitch
Dividing line (ivory)	1 stitch
Dividing line (brown-black)	1 stitch
Zigzag band	3 stitches
Dividing line (brown-black)	1 stitch
Dividing line (ivory)	1 stitch
Dividing line (red)	1 stitch
Arabesque border	45 stitches
Dividing line (red)	1 stitch
Dividing line (ivory)	1 stitch
Dividing line (brown-black)	1 stitch
Zigzag band	3 stitches
Dividing line (brown-black)	1 stitch
Dividing line (ivory)	1 stitch
Dividing line (red; field line)	1 stitch
Total width of border =	63 stitches

6. Stitch the small gold diamond at the center of the design, the star, and the enclosing diamond.

7. After you have established the center of the pattern, continue working the design from the lower right corner. Color the graph lightly with red and yellow pencils to define the design more clearly.

8. Continue stitching the outlines and then fill in the arabesques with gold, and the background with red yarn. Work the small additional motifs in blue and green.

9. Work the narrow zigzag guard bands. Fill in the red first, then stitch the gold line.

10. To establish the pattern in the main border: Put in the small squares indicated on the graph which repeat rightside up and upside down throughout the design.

With dark brown work the outlines as indicated.

With red, yellow, or blue yarn outline the large hooked motifs. Fill in the shapes with red, blue, and green.

Work the continuous ivory arabesque.

Work the background in dark blue.

11. Do not stitch any extra rows around the outer edge of the finished rug. Bind with red yarn.

Note: In addition to the narrow zigzag border, a wider leaf and vine guard band appears in Lotto rugs (figure 3–11). Include this pattern for a more elaborate design.

Design Ideas for Coordinate Patterns

Use portions of the field for an individual design (see figures 3–12, 3–13, and 3–14).

Make an all-over design using the border pattern (see figure 3–15).

Repeat the additional guard band as an all-over or floral stripe pattern.

3–12. Lower right portion of field.

3–13. Lower middle.

3–14. Center.

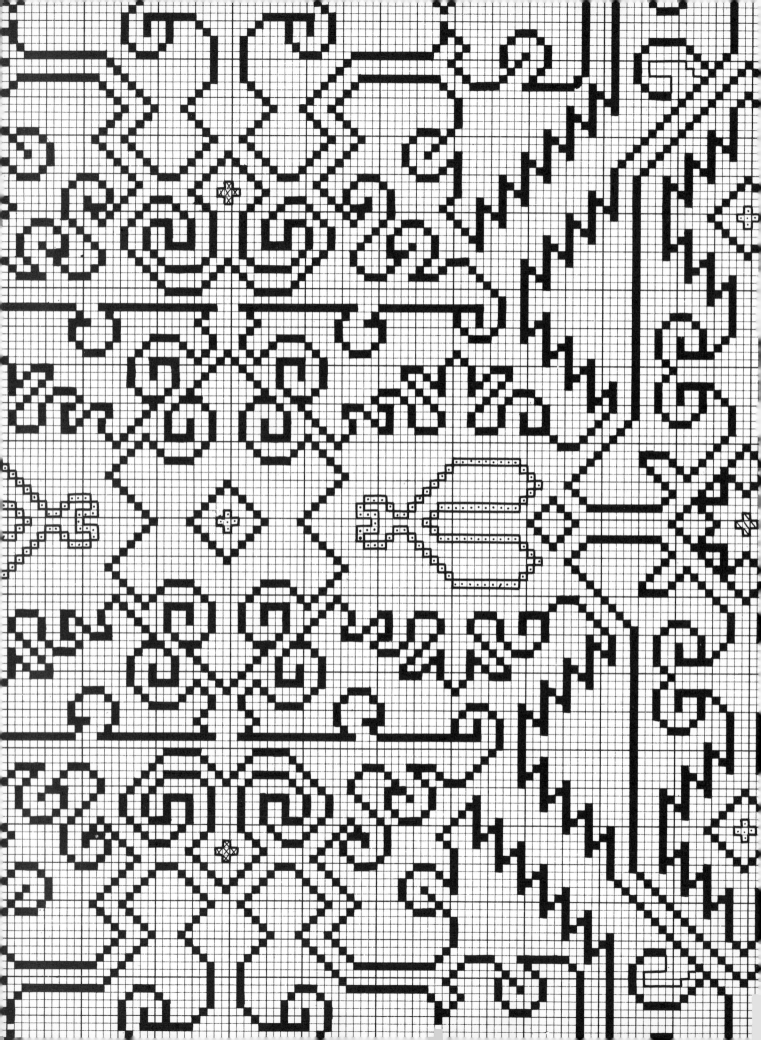

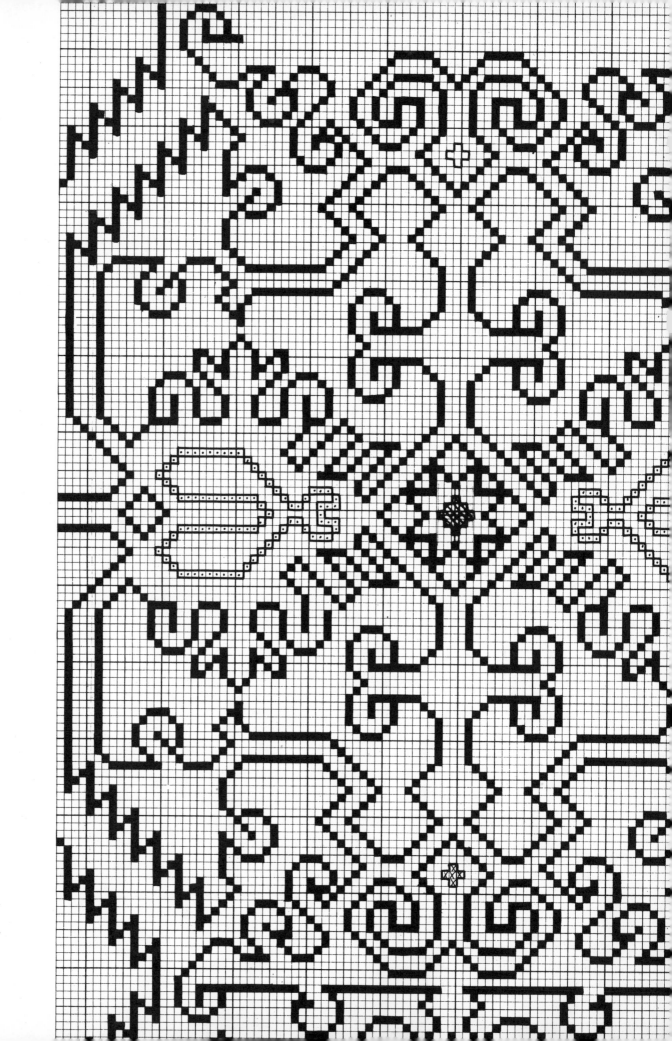

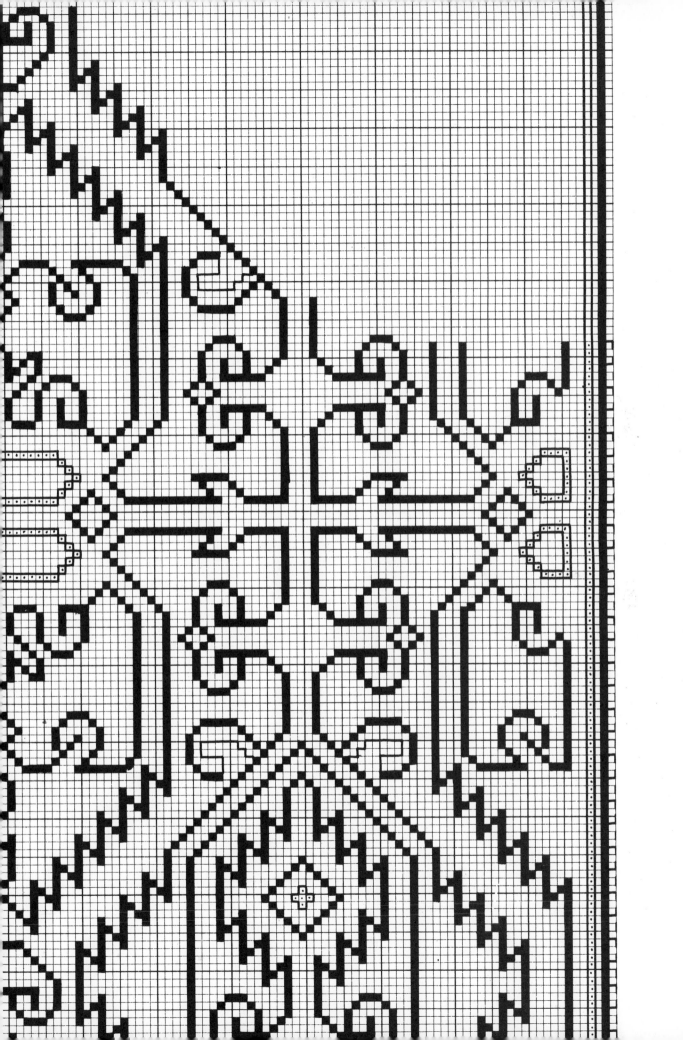

BERGAMA RUG
49″ by 79″ (125 cm × 200 cm) on #8 penelope canvas

If I were asked to choose a favorite rug from among the rugs in this book, I would hesitate to do so, because I find them all wonderful, each in its own way. But if I had to choose, I would select this one. It is the one I stitched myself; perhaps it has some aspects of a first love, since it is the design that started me on this project. The qualities I saw then are every bit as fresh now. In fact, having had the completed rug for a while, I find that its appeal has only increased with familiarity. It was a pleasure to work, and it is a pleasure to have and look at.

I think of this rug as a bridge between the old and the new. Its graphic clarity and balance appeal to modern tastes, yet the design harks back to early times. The double-octagon medallion is probably pre-Islamic. This motif is very much in the mainstream of classic Turkish rug design. It is also related to the motifs of carpets depicted in some of the paintings of Hans Holbein the Younger.

I have seen a number of versions of this design, but none more fully realized than this one. It is a village rug of a type much sought after today. It is named after a Turkish village on the site of Pergamon, the famous capital of Hellenistic times. The village may have been the place of origin, though the rug's history is now in dispute.

The colors in this rug are clear, strong, and vibrant, with a few tones in careful balance. What first strikes the eye in this bold design are the two white octagon medallions. Within each is a smaller red octagon containing a star-and-knot motif. Radiating from each side of the red octagons is a panel enclosing a hook design. The total effect is riveting and easy to grasp, but as we contemplate it, we notice subtleties and richness of variation, such as the latch hooks that engage the field in a negative and positive interplay, and the slightly turning rosettes at the corners of the field.

The compact, angular design of the field is set off by a simple but animated border. Its geometric shapes were probably based on floral forms. If this repeat were extended in all directions it would make a wonderful all-over design for a pillow or other small piece, even in colors that differ from those in the rug. This is a good way to use left-over materials.

The graph is different in some respects from the sample rug. I had only a brief opportunity to see and chart the original at the Metropolitan Museum of Art in New York before the rug became unavailable for viewing (until the Islamic galleries were opened). In the interim, I stitched the carpet. When I saw the original again I noticed discrepancies between it and my version. The graph and yarn colors indicated are closer to the original in scale and color than is the sample shown on the back of the jacket.

Color

Color	Principal Colors (8)		Auxiliary Colors (2)	
	Amount	Paternayan Yarn No.	Amount	Paternayan Yarn No.
dark brown	1 lb.	105		
ivory	1 lb.	136		
red	1½ lbs.	211	¼ lb.	205
dark blue	1 lb.	365	¼ lb.	334
blue	¼ lb.	330	¼ lb.	334
gold	½ lb.	419		
salmon	½ lb.	269		
violet	½ lb.	123		

The brownish color seen in the sample rug is a violet that has faded. I have included in the listing a color closer to the original.

Use lighter shades of blue in the hooked motifs in the field to prevent the pattern from appearing too static. Note that many of the blue motifs in the border are outlined in red. This can be seen in the color plate on the back cover, though it is not indicated on the graph. Use this outline for a nice contrast.

Directions

1. Prepare a piece of #8 penelope canvas 55″ by 85″ (140 cm by 216 cm).

2. Mark the corresponding (heavy) graph lines.

3. Mark the center horizontal and vertical threads of the canvas.

4. Mark the outer edge of the design. The graph thread count is 391 by 631. Horizontally, there are 195 stitches on either side of the center thread. Vertically, there are 315 stitches on either side of the center thread.

5. Mark the dividing lines of the border. Start from the outer edge, using the following table.

Outer edge	**1 stitch**
Barber's pole band	2 stitches
Dividing line	**1 stitch**
Running dog band	5 stitches
Dividing line	**1 stitch**
Barber's pole band	2 stitches
Dividing line	**1 stitch**

Geometric border	45 stitches
Dividing line	**1 stitch**
Barber's pole band	2 stitches
Dividing line	**1 stitch**
Running dog band	5 stitches
Dividing line	**1 stitch**
Barber's pole band	2 stitches
Dividing line (field line)	**1 stitch**
Total width of border =	71 stitches

6. Outline the four star-and-octagon motifs, that are centered on the horizontal axis. Place two single stitches between them and a cross and a single stitch at each end.

7. Outline the star-and-knot motif and fill in with colored yarn. Outline the smaller octagon, the octagon panels, and the large octagon on the lower half of the design.

8. Outline the octagons and rosettes at the bottom of the field. Work the four small diamonds.

9. Put in the hooked devices in the eight panels radiating from the central octagon in the large octagon medallion. The motifs in the horizontal and vertical panels repeat twice and those in the diagonal panels repeat four times. There are only three different motifs. The rug is symmetrical, and the upper and lower panels are worked in the same way. To see the design more clearly, color the graph lightly with colored pencils.

10. When the pattern is complete, fill in the remainder of the lower half of the design with colored yarn, using the Color Plate on the back of the jacket as a guide.

11. Work the narrow "running dog" border and the small bands of red and ivory stripes.

12. Put the two hooked motifs into the triangular panels at the center of the rug (figure 3–16). Follow the drawing in the graph, and color the graph lightly with colored pencils, using the color code and the sample rug as a guide.

13. Follow the graph and outline the large octagon at the top of the design. Put in the motifs in the panels. Keep them in the same position as those in the bottom half.

14. Continue working the upper portion of the rug.

15. When the field and the inner guard band are complete, work the border. Although there is an alternate red-and-blue pattern in the lower segment of the border, the remainder of the sequence is randomly worked. The border in the graph is symmetrical and continuous, whereas in the sample rug (and in the original) the side panels extend to the top of the rug. (The weavers started at the bottom of the rug, and often let the top end arbitrarily.)

16. Complete the outermost guard bands.

17. Stitch an extra row of red around the outermost edge of the finished rug. Bind with red yarn.

Note: There will be slight differences between the drawing in the graph and the sample rug. The rug in the color plate is 60″ by 84″ on #10 mono canvas. The rug as graphed is 49″ by 78″ on #8 canvas, closer in scale to the original.

Design Ideas for Coordinate Patterns

Use the star-and-knot motifs of the central medallions for a repeating design, either with or without the enclosing octagons. One motif could also be used individually for a smaller piece, such as a pillow.

Use the large octagon medallion individually.

Create an all-over design using the border pattern.

Make an all-over pattern using the rosettes at the corners of the field.

red
dark blue
blue
gold
salmon
violet

103

dark brown
red
gold
blue

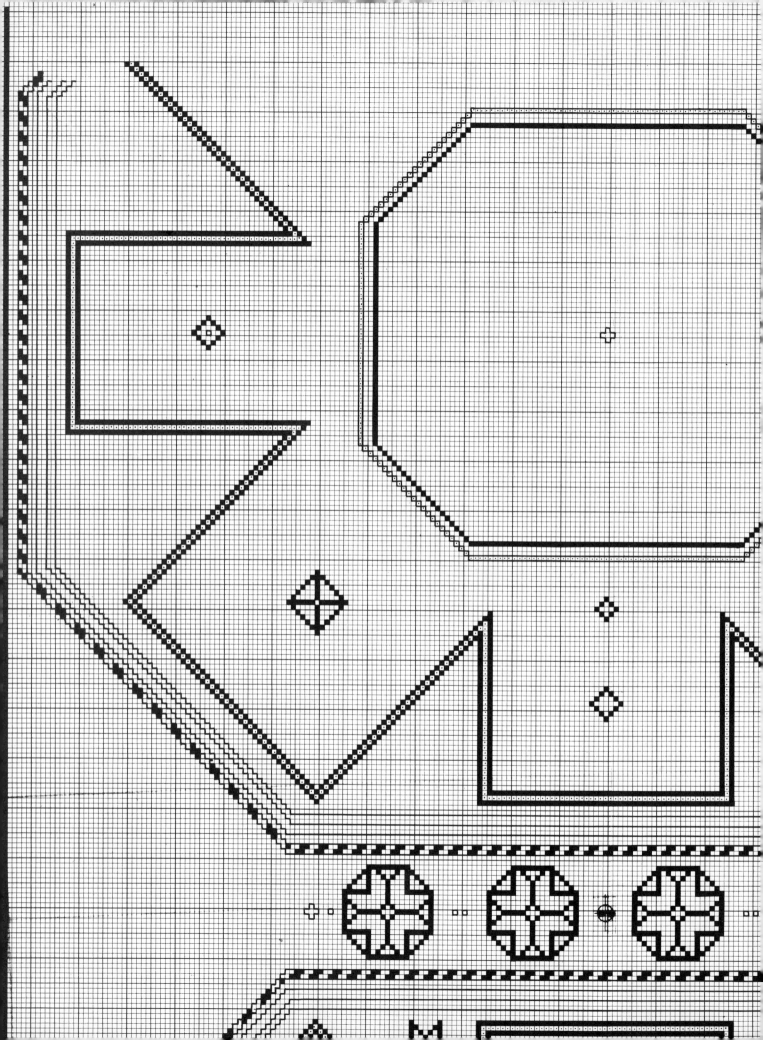

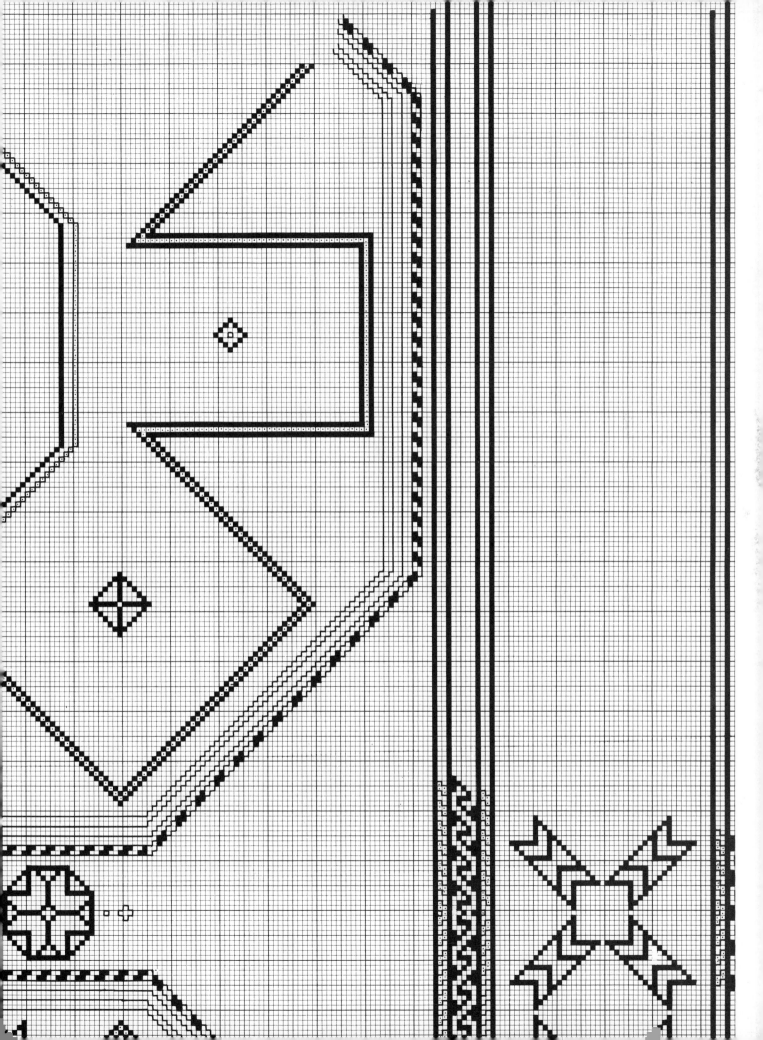

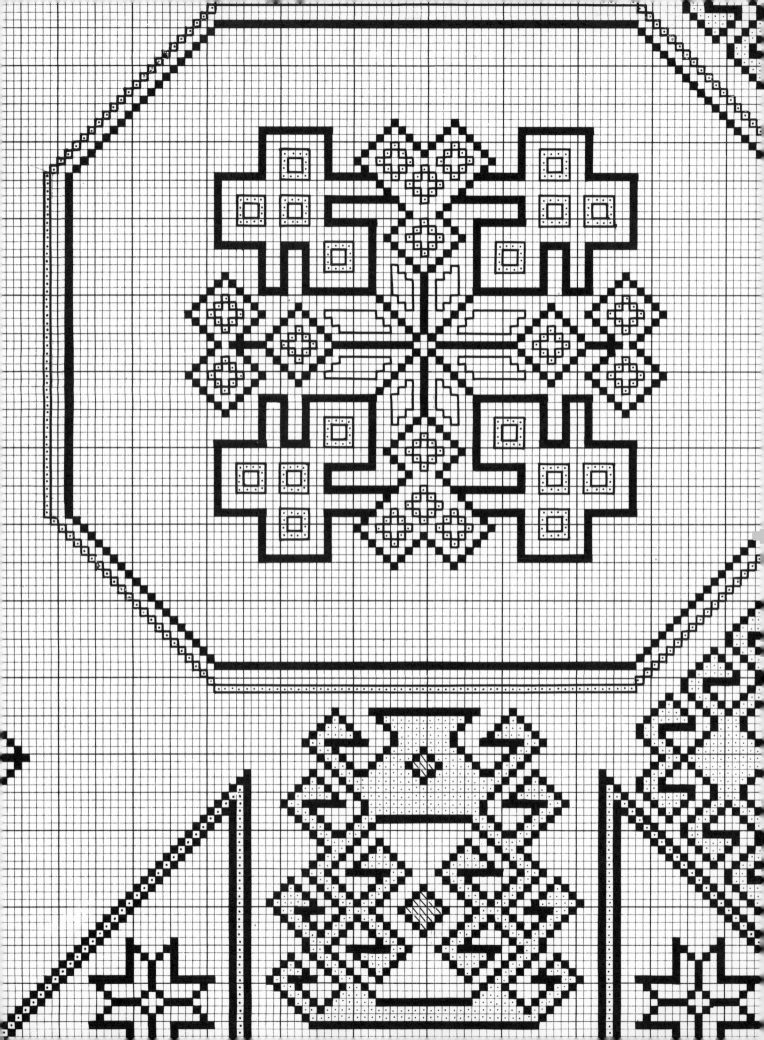

TURKISH MAT

25″ by 38 ½″ (64 cm × 98 cm) on #8 penelope canvas

Some of the pleasantest time spent in research for this book was when I was able to view the rugs at the storerooms of the Metropolitan Museum of Art in New York City. They are stored rolled up, and each in turn was unrolled for me on a tabletop. They are too large to be unrolled completely, so I viewed them piecemeal. The original of this rug was small enough to have been entirely unrolled, and it was a magical experience for me. Its colors literally shone. The rug seemed larger than its actual size because of the completeness of the design.

It was so indelibly imprinted upon my memory that the next day I was able to draw the entire graph working from notes made during my visit. I still have a particular fondness for this rug, and I have noticed that when others see it for the first time, they use adjectives such as *sweet* or *charming* in an equally affectionate way. Of all the rugs in this collection, it is the closest to the original, a country village rug that is quite possibly one of a kind.

In general, Oriental rugs, of whatever size, are space-filled designs; there are few areas in a given design that one could call "empty." Yet with all the wealth of detail, the designs are almost never confusing. This rug is a good example of a lot of detail fitted into a small area in a very orderly way. A large medallion occupies the center of the field and contains a heavily outlined eight-pointed star from which eight tree motifs radiate. From the top and bottom of the yellow medallion spring two palmettes, enclosing small shrubs. From the spandrels in the corners of the field are sprouting, budlike forms. Amid all this activity there is still more—two different kinds of geometric rosettes surround the central motif. The narrow border is filled with bright flowers on a green ground, continuing the theme of the field and enhancing the impression of burgeoning life and energy.

Because there are no outlines on most of the motifs, working this design requires more concentration than do some other patterns in this book. Approach the work in an unhurried way. You could create an outline by first stitching the outermost row of a shape before filling it in. Or, you could work from one 10 by 10 area of graph boxes to another. By this method you would complete the stitches of one 10-stitch-by-10-stitch area, and then go on to an adjacent one. Or, you may find a combination of the two methods is best for you. Once you find a comfortable approach, the work will proceed easily.

Color

Color	Principal Colors (7)		Auxiliary Colors (5)	
	Amount	Paternayan Yarn No.	Amount	Paternayan Yarn No.
red	¾ lb.	210		
light red	12 strands	245		
yellow	3 oz.	445	3 oz.	433
blue	1 oz.	365		
green	2 oz.	340	15 strands	367
dark brown	¼ lb.	112	2 oz.	210
ivory	3 oz.	136	25 strands	492

In this rug, the shapes are small enough for you to omit shading and still retain the same quality. The light red 245 is used only for the center star.

Directions

1. Prepare a piece of #8 penelope canvas 31″ by 45″ (77 cm by 114 cm). (This canvas is available in a 36″ width.)

2. Mark the corresponding (heavy) graph lines.

3. Mark the center horizontal and vertical threads of the canvas.

4. Mark the outer edge of the design. The graph thread count is 197 by 305. Horizontally, there are 98 stitches on either side of the center thread. Vertically, there are 152 stitches on either side of the center thread.

5. Mark the dividing lines of the border. Start from the outer edge, using the following table.

Outer edge (brown)	**1 stitch**
Dividing line (red)	**1 stitch**
Dividing line (brown)	**1 stitch**
Zigzag band	5 stitches
Dividing line (brown)	**1 stitch**
Dividing line (red)	**1 stitch**
Rosette border	9 stitches
Dividing line (red)	**1 stitch**
Dividing line (brown)	**1 stitch**
Zigzag band	5 stitches
Dividing line (brown; field line)	**1 stitch**
Total width of border =	27 stitches

6. Work the light red, green, and brown shapes in the center.

7. Outline the corner spandrels.

8. Continue working the central medallion. Use red and blue fine-point markers to indicate the position of the small dots throughout the medallion. These will serve as a guide when you are stitching the large shape.

9. Outline the small geometric motifs in the field.

10. Fill in the remainder of the field, using the Color Plate on the front of the jacket and the color code as a guide.

11. Work the zigzag guard bands and the main border. From left to right (clockwise), the color sequence of the rosettes is: yellow, red, ivory, and brown.

12. A red border was stitched around the perimeter as an equivalent to the multiple rows of wrapping vis-ible on the original rug. If you choose to omit these extra rows, stitch a single row of red, and bind in the same color.

Design Ideas for Coordinate Patterns

Use the central portion of the medallion on a yellow field.

Use the eight-pointed star in the center of the medallion individually for a smaller piece or repeated for a larger piece.

Make an all-over geometric pattern of the rosettes of the border.

Create a diamond using the corner spandrels of the field. Place the rosettes and lozenges of the field within.

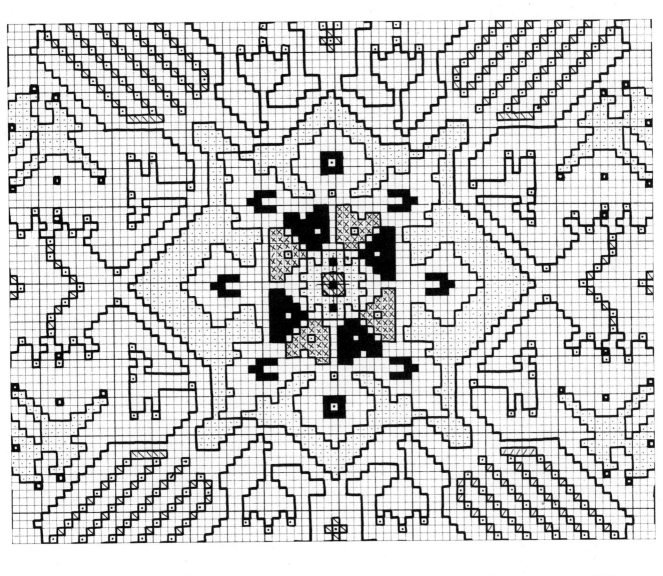

	dark brown		green
	ivory		gold
	red		blue

115

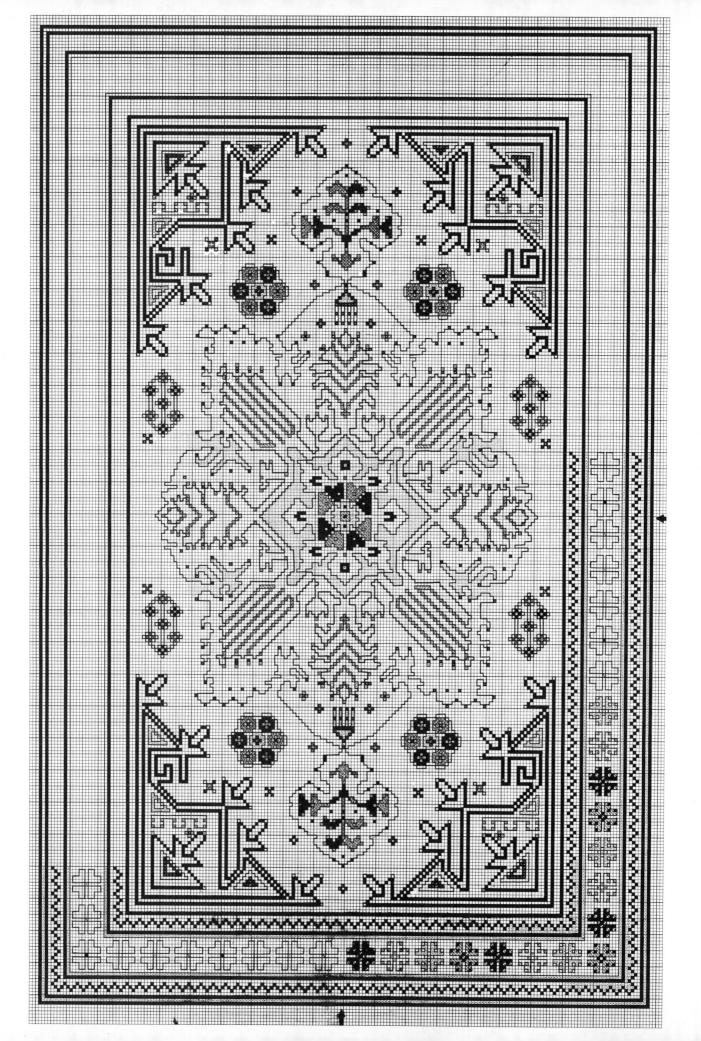

4. FINISHING

When all the stitching is done, including extra rows around the outside, the needlepoint must be finished to become a completed rug. Blocking, hemming, and binding, in that order, are the three steps that accomplish this.

Blocking is done to resquare the needlepoint, which is usually thrown out of shape when it is being stitched. To block, tack the rug face down to a flat surface, with the corners and sides squared. Then dampen it thoroughly. When it dries, it will retain the squared shape.

Hemming and binding produce a neat and attractive edge and prevent the rug from unraveling. In hemming, miter the corners, then fold the extra canvas under toward the back and gently tack it to the needlework. Then bind the narrow fold of unworked mesh with yarn, using a simple binding or wrapping stitch.

The appearance of your finished needlepoint will differ somewhat from a hand-knotted rug because the top, bottom, and both sides will be uniform. On a woven Oriental rug, the sides are wrapped to produce a selvedge during the weaving process. When the weaving is completed, the ends (top and bottom) are cut to form fringes. In many old rugs where the fringes have worn away, restorers bind those ends, giving an appearance similar to the binding of a needlepoint rug.

Blocking

When blocking is accomplished, the design will come sharply into focus, like a television image that has been askew and is then properly adjusted.

You will need a work surface that is larger than the entire canvas. The floor or a tabletop are good, if you do not mind stapling into them. You may obtain a plywood sheet, half an inch thick (1.27 cm) and four feet wide by eight feet long (122 cm × 244 cm) at a lumberyard. If your canvas is wider than four feet, you can place two narrower plywood sheets, each thirty inches (76 cm) wide, together. The lumberyard will cut them for you. This will match the sixty-inch (152-cm) canvas, and the edge can be used as a guide in blocking. (You may also want them to trim the length of the board or boards to make them less cumbersome.)

Using toweling and cotton sheeting or unbleached muslin to pad the board is optional but preferable. Toweling will help absorb and hold the moisture, and the muslin will provide a smooth, clean surface on which to place your rug.

You will also need:

- A staple gun with five-sixteenths-inch staples, or a hammer and rustproof tacks.
- A square, preferably a large one, such as a carpenter's square, T-Square, or large triangle. You *can* square the rug using only a tape measure or yardstick if you begin with a squared board, but a square is very helpful.
- A sprayer that can be filled with water, or a hose with a nozzle that can be adjusted to a fine spray.
- Pliers and a screwdriver for removing the tacks or staples.

Since the rug will need three days to a week to dry (depending on the weather) before it can be removed from the blocking surface, place it where it can remain undisturbed for at least that period of time. Now you are ready to begin blocking.

1. Pad the face of the board with towels and cotton sheeting, or unbleached muslin.

2. Place the rug face down on the blocking surface. If you are using a squared board, place one corner of the rug near a corner of the board; you will use the sides of the board itself as a guide. Otherwise, draw or tape on the blocking surface a rectangle that corresponds with the dimensions of the canvas.

3. Using the edge as a guide, staple or tack one long side of the rug to the board. Follow the straight line closely with the edge of the canvas. Staple or tack through the canvas one inch from the needlepoint, with the staples or tacks two inches apart.

4. Now, pulling the short side of the canvas just enough to get it into shape, staple or tack as before, starting at the attached corner and working your way to the other end. You almost certainly will have to pull—you can use a pair of pliers. Don't pull more than necessary, and don't worry if wrinkles appear in the rug, as long as the edges you are stapling or tacking are straight.

5. Staple or tack the second short side. Begin by aligning and stapling or tacking the free corner. If you can't quite reach this mark, that is all right; this is intended only to hold the corner close to its proper position while you staple the side. The staples or tacks at this corner can be removed later if further adjustment is required.

6. Starting at the fastened side, staple or tack the second short side in the same manner as before. As you approach the corner you have just fastened, you will in all likelihood have to remove the staples or tacks and make a slight adjustment.

7. Before fastening the last (long) side, measure the

length and width and make sure the corners of the needlepoint are squared. Both corners of the fastened (long) side should be the same distance from the one already fastened. A good way to do this side is to work from the center of the line toward each corner. This will avoid bunching. Smooth the edge out as you go, and if you have to make adjustments, do so on this side rather than on those already squared.

8. Wet the rug thoroughly and evenly with a fine spray. This releases the sizing of the canvas, which will then dry into the new squared shape; water will not harm the rug. The rug should be thoroughly dampened but not dripping.

9. Allow the rug to dry completely. Then, using a screwdriver or a pair of pliers, remove the staples or tacks. If the rug had been badly out of shape, however, do not remove the staples at this point, but repeat the dampening and drying procedure, and then remove the fasteners.

Hemming

1. Trim the unworked canvas to a 2-inch (5-cm) margin all around (figure 4–1).

2. Trim each corner diagonally within 1-inch of the stitching (figure 4–1).

3. With the back of the work facing you, fold in each corner, leaving approximately two rows (an eighth of an inch) free for binding (figure 4–2).

4. Flap the adjoining sides over the folded corner (figure 4–3), and whip hems into a mitered corner, using carpet or button-stitching thread (figure 4–4).

5. Use the same thread and a back stitch to sew the four hems to the underside of the work. Do not pick up more than wool on the back of your rug when you sew the hems to it. You do not want the thread to show on the surface of your work.

6. Turn your work over. There should be two rows of unstitched canvas showing around the edge on the front (see figure 4–5 for mono and figure 4–6 for penelope). Press the hems and the corners on the back of the work. You are now ready to bind your rug.

Binding

Among the most singular characteristics of the original rugs were the finishing of the edges and ends. The method of doing them usually followed rigid local traditions, so that even if the design was borrowed from elsewhere, the edges and ends looked like those of the area where it was made. There was great variation between areas: the binding or "wrapping" might be a solid color or stripes; it might be thick and round or wide and flat; sometimes multicolored threads were

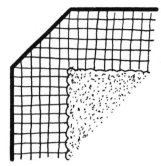

4–1. Trim the canvas to a two-inch margin along the edges, and the corners to within one inch of the needlepoint (shown schematically).

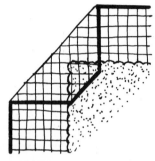

4–2. With the back of the work facing you, fold in each corner. Leave approximately two rows free for binding.

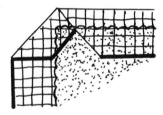

4–3. Flap the adjoining sides over the folded corner.

4–4. Whip hems into a mitered corner, using carpet or button stitching thread.

used. In binding your needlepoint there is room for your own personal preference. All the sample rugs were finished with a solid-color binding, but there is no reason you can't have a striped binding or one stitched with multicolored strands of wool.

Binding is done with a double thread thirty inches (75 cm) long. To thread a needle for binding, follow this procedure:

1. Take a full skein of wool. Cut it only once. Each

strand of yarn will be twice as long (about sixty inches (150 cm)) as those you have been using.

2. Thread the needle and pull it to the center of the strand. With the point of the needle, stitch through both strands hanging from the eye, as close to it as possible.

3. Draw the needle through, and smooth the threads. The double thread will not slip and it will be the proper length (about thirty inches [75 cm]).

4. Work the binding stitch over the two rows of mesh showing at the edge of your needlepoint (figure 4–5, mono and figure 4–6, penelope). Always work with the wrong side of the canvas facing you, and from left to right.

5. Begin working at a corner. Fasten your wool in the backs of some stitches under the hem. Bring the needle up to the right side of the needlepoint and begin binding. Pass the needle over two horizontal threads in such a way that every adjacent hole is filled. The stitch slants from the lower right to the upper left (figure 4–7).

6. Continue binding, making a neat, even spiral and letting the yarn untwist as you work. Keep an even tension; uneven stitches will make a wavy edge. When starting or ending, run the yarn through some stitches under the hem, or through the row of binding. Don't knot the yarn.

7. When you reach the corner, turn the canvas ninety degrees. If you cannot cover the point, color the canvas with a waterproof marking pen the same color as the yarn.

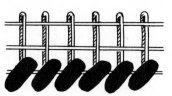

4–5. Two rows of canvas showing at the edge of the needlepoint on mono mesh.

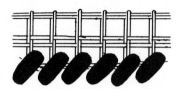

4–6. Two rows of canvas showing at the edge of the needlepoint on penelope mesh.

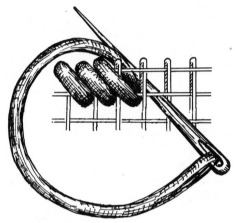

4–7. The binding stitch. Each stitch slants from the lower right to the upper left.

5. DISPLAY AND CARE

Not everyone may be interested in stitching an Oriental rug, but nearly everyone would be glad to have one. The impulse to possess them is similar to that which led to their creation: the desire to be surrounded by beauty.

With their bold colors and attractive patterning, Oriental rugs were accorded a primary role in their original surroundings; there were few competing forms of decoration where rugs were made. In the West, they fit very comfortably into even those surroundings where there is much else to catch the eye, and in so doing they have lost none of their power.

In the last thirty years, Oriental rugs have grown from objects acquired by only a few knowledgeable collectors or wealthy families to well-deserved recognition as full-fledged works of art. Even the more "folkish" types, the village and nomadic rugs, are highly prized today as examples of a quickly disappearing art. Museum and private collections of rugs have grown, books on Oriental rugs abound, and an increasing number of scholars devote their attention to them exclusively.

Oriental rugs are so valuable these days that in a way having a needlepoint reproduction rather than an original is a plus. No one today would think of using a museum-quality piece, such as the originals of those illustrated in this book, as a floor covering. But you can enjoy a needlepoint version, experiencing it as it was originally intended. Often the owner of a valuable rug will not even chance the deterioration that might come from having it on display, preferring to keep it in storage, to be taken out only on special occasions. One collector has even asked me to chart some of the rugs she owns so that she can stitch them and be able to see them daily.

Displaying Your Rug

The rugs in this book will look beautiful on the floor in virtually any room, and the needlepoint will wear very well. But remember, the people who made the original rugs would never have walked on them in footwear comparable to our street shoes; these rugs, too, deserve a certain amount of respect.

Do not place the rug directly on a bare hardwood floor. It will require some padding underneath (I suggest sheet rubber slab). Cut the padding slightly smaller all around than the carpet. To hold it in place, sew four strips of natural-fiber cloth tape diagonally across each corner of the rug. Insert the padding into these tabs.

Another way to display an Oriental rug is to place it on a flat-topped piece of furniture such as a table or chest. Historically, in Europe and America, this was common, as can be seen in old paintings. Until the late nineteenth century, Oriental rugs were seldom used any other way.

Today, valuable rugs are most commonly seen on the wall, as they are shown in museums. A good rug makes a beautiful "picture," and it is well protected in this way. Rugs should always be hung vertically, i.e., not from the selvedge, because the warp threads of the canvas are stronger and hang better than the weft threads. There are several ways to mount a rug on the wall safely:

A Sleeve: Sew a cotton sleeve to the back of the rug just below the top hem. Make the sleeve wide enough to accommodate a rod, and stitch the top of the sleeve to the rug with cotton thread, being careful that the stitches do not show on the front. Make sure that they catch both the horizontal and vertical threads of the basket-weave stitch on the back. Then insert a rod of wood or metal through the sleeve so that an end of the rod sticks out at either side. Attach the rod to the wall by brackets or suspended it on cord or wire from hooks secured in the ceiling.

Rings: You can use metal or plastic rings as long as they are not attached directly to the rug. Sew the rings onto a two- or three-inch (7.5-cm) strip of cotton tape; then stitch the tape to the back of the rug as for a sleeve. Pass a rod through the rings, and suspend it from brackets or hooks in the wall or ceiling.

Velcro: You can use Velcro, but it must be sewn to cotton tape or cloth, which is then sewn onto the carpet. The rug is then mounted by stitching the matching piece of Velcro onto unbleached muslin tightly stretched over a canvas stretcher frame. If the rug is rolled or folded for storage, the Velcro should be removed, because it will cause uneven tension on the rug's surface.

And remember: Never directly tack or nail a textile to a wall, and never hang any textile in direct sunlight or near a source of heat.

Caring for Your Rug

If you had a valuable textile for which you paid thousands of dollars, you would make sure to take very good care of it. Well, you *do* have its equivalent—the needlepoint rug you have just completed (just total your working time at a modest rate of pay, plus materials). A handmade embroidery of this kind will be valued by others as well. There is no reason why it cannot be kept in good enough condition to be passed on to the next generation—you can be quite sure they will want it. People have a tendency to want to preserve what is carefully made by hand, and in your way you have just added to the world's store of such objects. Your needlepoint rug is sturdy enough to be used *and* kept in good condition, if you follow these procedures for caring for it.

Cleaning

Vacuuming is the easiest way to clean your rug. Lay it on a clean surface, and vacuum gently, using the small, smooth-edged attachment. Reduce the suction by opening the vents, or use a low power setting. Clean the surface the rug is lying on before turning the rug over to vacuum the other side.

Wet cleaning may be employed if the rug needs to be more thoroughly cleaned. Use water and a mild detergent solution. If you used marking pens in making the rug, be sure that they were waterproof. You can test each color on the rug by applying a few drops of water, blotting with a clean white cloth, then applying a few drops of detergent solution to the same area and blotting again. If there is no color on the cloth, proceed with wet cleaning. There are commercial cleaning establishments that do wet cleaning with water and a neutral detergent, and you may want to use one of these, or you may wish to do it yourself.

For wet cleaning, the rug must be completely submerged in a clean container; a bathtub will do fine. Fill with enough water (seventy to eighty degrees Fahrenheit) (21°–27° Celsius) to cover the rug. For each gallon of water add one-half ounce of detergent. Use a neutral detergent such as Orvus WA paste (see mail order supplies) or a very mild dishwashing detergent such as Ivory liquid. If your area has hard water, it should be softened or filtered before you use it on your rug. Submerge the rug for no more than one hour, gently sponging the suds solution through the rug. Don't scrub, wring, or rub. Try to keep the rug as flat as possible. Rinse at least four times, or until no trace of suds remains.

After washing, the rug will have to be reblocked. Remove the stitches holding the hem (not the binding), and open. (The hem can be restitched when the rug is dry.) Blot the wet rug with toweling or sheeting to absorb the excess moisture.

Storage

If you wish to store your rug, the best way to do so is to roll it up. Use a cardboard tube two (5 cm) to six inches (15 cm) in diameter and at least as long as the rug is wide. The tube should be sealed to prevent the acids in the cardboard from leaching through to the rug. For this use polyurethane sealer, available in any paint store. When the tube is dry, cover it with several layers of clean, unbleached muslin. After vacuuming both sides of the rug, lay it on a clean surface. Placing the tube across the width at one end, roll the rug very evenly, face out. Roll as straight as possible and avoid any slack (you may need help for this). When it is rolled, tie with cotton tape in several places and cover it with washed, unbleached muslin or cotton sheeting.

The rolled-up rug can be stored horizontally on a shelf. Or, a long rod can be inserted through the tube and used to support or hang it, keeping the weight off the rug itself. The rug should not be kept in a humid basement or a poorly insulated attic. Try to keep it within an even sixty-five to seventy degree Fahrenheit (18° to 24° Celsius) temperature range. Protect the rug carefully against the menace of moths and carpet beetles, which will attack the wool with relish. Mothballs or parachlorobenzene crystals are an effective control, but never place them directly on the rug; put them in small muslin bags suspended throughout the storage area.

And may you, and your children, and your children's children enjoy your rug for a long, long time.

MAIL-ORDER SOURCES

Yarn

Chatalbash Rug Co., Inc.
245 Fifth Avenue
New York, NY 10016
(Paternayan yarn, $\frac{1}{2}$ lb. minimum)

Canvas

Pearl Art & Craft Suppliers
2411 Hempstead Turnpike
East Meadow, NY 11554

Handwork Tapestries Inc.
144 B Allen Boulevard
Farmingdale, N.Y. 11735
(wholesale canvas—
10 yard minimum)

BIBLIOGRAPHY

General Works on Oriental Rugs

Denny, Walter B. *Oriental Rugs.* New York: Cooper-Hewitt Museum, 1979.
Dimand, M. S., and Jean Mailey. *Oriental Rugs in the Metropolitan Museum of Art.* New York: The Metropolitan Museum of Art, 1973.
Erdmann, Kurt. *Seven Hundred Years of Oriental Carpets.* Translated by May H. Beattie and Hildegard Herzog. Berkeley and Los Angeles: University of California Press, 1970.
Hubel, Reinhard G. *The Book of Carpets.* New York: Praeger, 1970.
Schlosser, Ignaz. *The Book of Rugs Oriental and European.* New York: Bonanza, 1968.

Works on Types of Rugs

Ettinghausen, Richard, M. S. Dimand, Louise W. Mackie, and Charles Grant Ellis. *Prayer Rugs.* Washington, D.C.: Textile Museum, 1974.
Mackie, Louise W. *The Splendor of Turkish Weaving,* Washington, D.C.: Textile Museum, 1973.

Catalogs and Pamphlets

Bacharach, Jere L., and Irene A. Bierman. *The Warp and Weft of Islam.* Seattle: Henry Art Gallery, University of Washington, 1978.
Jones, J. McCoy, and Ralph S. Yohe. *Turkish Rugs.* Washington, D.C.: Textile Museum, 1968.
McMullen, Joseph V. *Islamic Carpets.* New York: Near Eastern Art Research Center, 1965.
Tschebull, R. *Kazak.* New York: Near Eastern Art Research Center and New York Rug Society, 1971.

Islamic Pattern

Künel, Ernst. *The Arabesque.* Translated by R. Ettinghausen. London: Oguz Press, 1976.
Wade, David. *Pattern in Islamic Art.* New York: Overlook Press, 1976.

METRIC EQUIVALENTS FOR YARN WEIGHTS

Metric equivalents are rounded off to the next highest gram.

1 oz.	=	29 gr.
2 oz.	=	57 gr.
3 oz.	=	86 gr.
$\frac{1}{4}$ lb.	=	114 gr.
$\frac{1}{4}$ lb.	=	227 gr.
$\frac{3}{4}$ lb.	=	341 gr.
1 lb.	=	454 gr.
$1\frac{1}{4}$ lbs.	=	567 gr.
$1\frac{1}{2}$ lbs.	=	681 gr.
2 lbs.	=	908 gr.
$2\frac{1}{2}$ lbs.	=	1134 gr.

COLOR EQUIVALENTS FOR D.M.C. AND BUCILLA YARNS

Paternayan Conversion Chart and Color Equivalents for D.M.C. and Bucilla Yarn.

Color	Paternayan yarn no.	D.M.C. yarn no.	Bucilla yarn no.	Color	Paternayan yarn no.	D.M.C. yarn no.	Bucilla yarn no.
dark brown	D-112 *421*	7535, 7526	192	medium blue	311 *510*	7296	217
	114 *450*	7535, 7526	192		314 *511*	7591	45
brown-black	105 *420*	7535	12, 192		334 *501*	7314	151
light brown	104 *440*	7499	191		330 *502*	7314	151
ivory	136 *455*(N)	7411	143	light blue	380 *512*	7592	108
	492 *444*	7579	48	dark green	D-516 *600*	7428	227
red	267 *860*	7446	166		340 *520*	7408, 7428	227
	210 *930*	7127	202	medium green	512 *601*	7394	226
	D-211 *930*	7127	202		367 *521*	7541	226
light red	274 *872*	7124	199	light green	560 *603*	7384	115
(salmon, pink)	269 *871*	7125	5	olive	583 *641*	7355	49
	245 *931*	7758	202		540 *651*	7394	237
	D-234 *931*	7207	207	dark gold	145 *441*	7477	161
dark red	D-207 *920*	7218	109		D-419 *731*	7444	157
	D-205 *920*	7218	109	gold	433 *751*	7505	160
maroon	201 *920*	7448	168		462 *442*	7494	251
dark blue	305 *570*	7925	218		466 *443*	7505	255
	D-323 *571*	7319	217	yellow	445 *752*	7473	241
	365 *500*	7319, 7296	217	violet	D-123 *471*	7226	196

As this book was going to press, Paternayan reorganized its color card. The numbers in the first column are the old numbers and the italic numbers in the second column are the new numbers. Some colors have been discontinued (D) and new colors have been added. Substitutions have been made where necessary.

APPENDIX: ORIGINAL RUGS

Shirvan Rug, 8 feet 8 inches by 3 feet 6 inches. First half of nineteenth century. In the collection of the Metropolitan Museum of Art, New York City. Catalog no. 169.

Caucasian Rug, 7 feet by 6 feet. Nineteenth century. In the McMullen Collection of the Metropolitan Museum of Art, New York City. Catalog no. 50.

Geometrical Kazak, 6 feet 6 inches by 8 feet 2 inches. In the collection of Fogg Art Museum, Harvard University, Cambridge, Massachusetts.

Lesghi Star, 4 feet 10 inches by 6 feet 10 inches. In the collection of Mr. and Mrs. Raul Tschebull.

Rug with Spots and Stripes, 6 feet by 10 feet. Late sixteenth or early seventeenth century. In the collection of the Textile Museum, Washington, D.C. Also based to some extent on an Anatolian rug, 5 feet 6 inches by 13 feet, in the collection of the Berlin Museum.

Turkish Prayer Rug, 3 feet 6¾ inches by 5 feet ¼ inch. Nineteenth century. In the McMullen Collection, Metropolitan Museum of Art, New York City. Catalog no. 93.

Transylvanian Rug, 4 feet 1 inch by 5 feet 7 inches. Seventeenth century. In the McMullen Collection, Metropolitan Museum of Art, New York City. Catalog no. 85.

Lotto Rug. An adaptation from several sources.

Bergama Rug, 4 feet 11 inches by 6 feet 3 inches. Nineteenth century. In the McMullen Collection, Metropolitan Museum of Art, New York City. Catalog no. 103.

Turkish Mat, 2 feet 9½ inches by 3 feet 2½ inches. Nineteenth century. In the McMullen Collection, Metropolitan Museum of Art, New York City. Catalog no. 117.

INDEX